Stop Throwing Money Away

Turn Clutter into Cash, Trash into Treasure— and Save the Planet While You're at It!

WITHDRAWN

JAMIE NOVAK

Published by John Wiley & Sons, Inc., Hoboken, New Jersey
Published simultaneously in Canada

For general information about our other products and services, please contact our Customer Care Department within the United States at (800) 762-2974, outside the United States at (317) 572-3993 or fax (317) 572-4002.

Wiley also publishes its books in a variety of electronic formats. Some content that appears in print may not be available in electronic books. For more information about Wiley products, visit our web site at www.wiley.com.

Library of Congress Cataloging-in-Publication Data:

Novak, Jamie.
    Stop throwing money away : turn clutter into cash, trash into treasure—and save the planet while you're at it! / Jamie Novak.
        p. cm.
    Includes index.
    ISBN 978-0-470-54900-1 (pbk.)
        1. Storage in the home. 2. Orderliness. 3. Thriftiness. I. Title.
    TX309.N687 2006
    648'.8—dc22
                                                                    2009041791

Printed in the United States of America

10   9   8   7   6   5   4   3   2   1

To you, someone who strives to create a rich, authentic and clutter-free life by finding and keeping more of your money, time, and energy!

Contents

Special Thanks

To my mom, Sue Novak, who taught me among many other lessons the benefits of keeping a bunch of paper towel tubes, margarine tubs, and shoeboxes on hand. To Dad and Stacey, who have taught me about caring for our planet and those who live on it, including each of their special cats. To my sisters, Brandy, Jessica, and Kristy, who picked up the phone every time I called to brainstorm ideas, even if they were in the middle of planning a wedding, having a cookout, or walking one of their children to school.

To Jessica Faust of Bookends, the most superfantastic literary agent any author could hope for. You're the literary version of eHarmony, consistently matching me with the project that's just right for me. To Christel Winkler, my editor at John Wiley & Sons, who believed in this book, and to the entire publishing team, each whom of contributed his or her own touch to make this book the best it could be. To my many Girl Scout leaders, including the spirited Mrs. Betty Riker, who taught me respect for the people and things around me. Because of her, I always leave an area better than it was when I found it. And to my Mastermind Group—Karyn Greenstreet, Pamela Wilson, Katherine Scott, and Susan Burger—like any great Mastermind Group, these ladies inspire, support, and challenge me. Thanks for the s'mores, ladies!

Welcome

Because you picked up this book, I have to ask, how would your life be different if you had an extra thousand dollars? Really think about it. Do you have a home repair that needs to be made or a child getting ready for college? Are you living paycheck to paycheck, or would you simply sleep better knowing you had a little more money in the bank? No matter where you are financially, we can all agree that an extra thousand bucks (or two or three) would be nice to have. So, whether you want to take a five-star vacation or save your home from foreclosure—or use that money for anything in between—this book is for you. You'll learn how to keep more money in your pocket and even make money by paring down your possessions. You'll also discover how to plug up your cash leaks by shopping at home.

I promise, *this is not your mother's financial planning book.* It is unlike any other organizing book on the market. Although I have financial planning in my background, my true love is organizing. I mean, I *really* love it, with an I-can't-wait-'til-morning-jump-out-of-bed-this-never-feels-like-work kind of love. As a result of my many years of working in clients' homes and meeting people who attend my workshops, I know one thing for certain. We're overwhelmed, and we feel hopeless about our state of disorganization. I mean, even *I* have had to clean up before company arrives, have misplaced the brand-new printer cartridge, and have bought another jar of marinara sauce when I already had more than I can use in a year sitting in the pantry. You never thought you'd hear an organizer admit that, huh? Well, it's true. I try, but I'm not perfect. That's what makes me the World's Most Relatable Organizer.

Why I Wrote This Book

Many years ago, while working for a large financial planning company, I often met my clients over their kitchen tables, and I noticed a common theme—clutter. Many clients had to move piles of papers off their tables before we could sit down. Then they had to sort through these piles to locate the necessary documents, such as bills or bank statements that we needed to complete their financial profiles. Not only were their filing cabinets overstuffed, but they had misplaced important paperwork and had lots of possessions they weren't using packed into their closets. As part of our appointment, I helped them figure out which papers to keep and which to shred. I helped them weed out their filing cabinets and bring order to their home offices. On our second appointment, when I returned with their financial profiles, they often realized that they were spending more money every month than they were bringing in, thus creating a shortfall.

Now, I'm no Suze Orman, but I know that's a problem. So I continued to help my clients clean up the clutter to find and keep more of their money. Sometimes we found $500 hiding in a wardrobe closet in the form of a bridal gown that they can sell, and other times we saved $5,000 in unnecessary storage rental fees because they were hoarding—I mean, housing— items they could no longer remember or identify. It was exciting for me to be part of their transformations from being overwhelmed to being organized and from being cash poor to cashing in. That's when I officially hung out my shingle as the World's Most Relatable Organizer.

From the many clients I've had over the years, I learned that there are four ways our clutter makes us poor. (Real names and identifying details have been changed to protect the cluttered):

1. **We can't find what we own, so we simply buy more.** Take, for example, Jennifer, whom you'll meet. She's a single professional and has bought more than her fair share of jeans and black turtlenecks because the ones she already owns are missing or in the laundry.

2. **We hold on to items of sellable value.** Kristin is newly married and fairly certain she'll never use the pasta maker that someone gave her as a gift, yet she's renting storage to hold on to it, just in case.

3. **We don't repurpose what we already own; we simply buy new.** Tracey, a married mom of two, has been known to throw glass jars into the recycling bin just before she heads out to buy glass vases for fresh flowers.

4. **We allow clutter-cash traps to go unattended.** Maryann, a married self-employed professional who is

a year away from having an empty nest, has admitted to missing the filing deadline on more than one scholarship application.

Half-and-Half Organizing: The Solution to Your Clutter Problem

From this day forward, you'll take a new approach to conquering the chaos in your home: half-and-half organizing. You'll make money by paring down what you own by half; then you'll plug your cash leaks by shopping at home. You'll learn to repurpose items you already own, instead of buying new. You can save hundreds of dollars a year by simply organizing your clutter-cash traps and selling the clutter for big profits.

Half-and-half organizing is *not* an all-or-nothing kamikaze technique. It can be tempting to think that you either have to de-clutter every room in your home in one weekend or you might as well not do anything at all. Those of us who fall into the perfectionist category often feel that if we can't do something right, we won't do it at all. But this project is too large to tackle all at once, so you'll start out in small, bite-size pieces, and before you know it, you'll be richer *and* more organized.

Consider the first pass through your home to be a rough draft. You can always go back and do more or perfect the project in your spare time. For now, you simply have to do a little at a time and keep it up until it's done.

This book will help you if:

- You find yourself embarrassed, overwhelmed, or feeling hopeless about the clutter.

- You don't know where to start or are not sure what to do first to get organized.

- You're busy, you procrastinate, or you are waiting to do a perfect job of de-cluttering.

- You need support, motivation, or to be held accountable, or you simply want a few more good ideas.

- You want more money in your pocket and less chaos in your life.

You will not find extensive worksheets to track your expenses for a month here, and you certainly won't hear cliché advice like "Pay yourself first" and "Freeze your credit cards, literally." You need some kick-butt ideas that really work so that you can finally achieve financial freedom. This book will be your lifestyle change.

I'm not here to tell you what to do with your money or what is and is not "necessary" spending. I won't help you craft a budget or balance your checkbook. I'm here to guide you through the moneyizing process. "Moneyizing" is what you will accomplish when your organizing efforts put more money in your pocket. To help make the process easier you'll record notes and key points, answer questions, and track your progress in a half-and-half journal. Start off your new routine by shopping at home to locate a spiral-bound notebook that you can use to keep your journal.

Half-and-Half Organizing Rules

- **Use it this week or don't buy it yet.** No sense spending money before it's absolutely necessary. You might change your mind, and then you'll have to find a place to store the new item until you do need it.

- **Shop from home, and reuse (almost) everything twice.** Before heading out to the store to purchase a new item, check around your own home to see if you already have it or have something you can substitute for it.

- **Pare down by half.** The goal is to let go of 50 percent in each area of your home. If you own thirty CDs find a new home for at least fifteen of them. Give them away or sell them. Do you have two ice cream scoops in the utensil drawer? Let one go.

- **One new item in, two of the old items out.** If you follow the old rule "one in one out," then you'll only maintain your clutter, not lessen it. Instead try "one in, two out." So for every new pair of jeans, two old pairs of pants head out the door.

- **Touch a paper twice.** The old school of organizing thought says "Touch a paper once." The idea is that when you pick up the paper, you should address it immediately: throw it out, file it, take action on it if you need to, but get it off your desk now. I've found that I can never handle all of that with just one touch. I have to touch it twice: once to find out what it is and put it in its home, another time to process it, file it, shred it, and so on.

And the big question to ask yourself about everything: *Is this absolutely necessary?*

Am I Wrong?

We see it on home-makeover shows all the time, but you tell me—how much financial sense does it make to hire an organizer at $75 an hour to help you clean out the stuff in your basement (empty shoeboxes, old tote bags, trunks, and so on), only to then buy decorative "organizing" boxes for $10 or more apiece and a chest of drawers for $80 to use for organizing?

Uh, hello, you just tossed out perfectly good boxes and trunks, which, in all honesty, make a perfect storage option when they're stacked. You wasted hours of time, rebought things you already owned, and paid someone about $300 to do it. At that rate, you'll *never* reach your financial goals!

I became the first organizer to say out loud, "Keep it. Don't toss it!" You can repurpose it, reuse it, sell it, or, at the very least, share it and take the tax deduction. Why would you waste it? My mission became teaching people how to clean up and get rich, how to organize with the purpose of saving and making money.

Maybe it's the Girl Scout in me, but I have a hard time tossing out perfectly useful stuff. Just because it did not come from the "right" store or was not originally intended to do a certain job does not mean that it won't work. In most cases, the improvised item works fine or, at least, is more fun.

As I sit at my desk typing this introduction, my pens are sitting in a yellow pen cup on the right-hand side of my desk. Is it a new, fancy, rotating-type of desk organizer? No, it is the pen cup I made with my mother when I was about nine years old. We needed a pen cup for our kitchen to keep the pens in by the phone. We could have gotten into the car, driven to the store, and bought one for about $10, but, instead, Mom inspired the inner crafter in me. She opened a tin can of corn, saved the corn to serve with dinner, rinsed the can out, and had an instant pen cup.

We took it a step further and wrapped the can in cheery yellow construction paper to match the kitchen. Then I was allowed to decorate it with stickers and aromatic markers—you know, the kind where the red smells just like ripe strawberries? My mom and I spent time together, we reused an object we already had around the house, and I have that pen cup to this day. Sure, the yellow is not as bright and a few of the stickers have fallen off, but that does not affect the cup's functionality.

To me, that sounds much better than driving to a crowded store simply to plunk down hard-earned money on a cheap pen cup. My mother is no longer with me, but I still have the memory of spending that time with her. Every time I see that pen cup, it makes me smile, which is something that a UPC symbol–bearing, store-bought cup could never do.

So, if you've ever said out loud or to yourself:

- I forgot I had this.
- I know it's here somewhere.
- I'm too busy to stop and get organized.
- I have papers stacked on every surface.
- I should have my financial matters more in order.
- I know I'd have more money if I were more organized.

Then you don't need to simply organize, you need to moneyize!

My Promise to You

I can't swear that you'll make a million-dollar discovery in the back of your closet, but I can promise that by following the advice in this book, you'll finally break through the barrier of your clutter and put yourself back in control of your finances. You'll be motivated to take action, having gained the wisdom, strength, and courage to create a rich, clutter-free life. And you'll have fun doing it.

Today is the day! The time to learn the secrets behind half-and-half organizing is now.

So, check your perfectionism at the door, and stop comparing yourself to others. This is *your* journey toward organization and financial freedom. Whether your Christmas tree is still up and it's June; you have piles of paper, mail, and bills to be filed, and the file drawer won't open; or you can't get your car into the garage—no matter where you are starting from, you simply have to begin. I'm right here with you.

Good Terms to Remember

Seven s's

1. Store items you want to keep.

2. Save the planet by recycling items you don't want and can't sell or give away.

3. Sell items that have cash value.

4. Share items that someone else can use.

5. Shred sensitive documents.

6. Swap items you don't use for something you will use.

7. Set your clutter free!

Brownie mix method   A process to organizing that is just as simple as baking brownies from a mix.

CAM score   Your clutter and money score, which will be determined by taking a ten-question quiz at the end of this chapter.

CASH   Collect the clutter, Appraise the articles, Sell the stuff, Have a rich life.

Clutter quotient   The real price you pay for any new item you buy or for the items you already own.

Curbside treasure   An item of value discarded by the side of the road, which you then pick up and reuse.

CUTE   <u>C</u>an't <u>u</u>se <u>t</u>his, <u>e</u>ver!

Dollar sign moment   A lightbulb moment when you realize you'd prefer to save the money, time, and energy, rather than to accumulate more clutter.

Ditto phenomenon   The mysterious way that items multiply when placed on flat surfaces or in dark closets.

GPS   <u>G</u>etting your <u>p</u>riorities <u>s</u>traight.

Half-and-half organizing   Make money by paring down what you own by half and plugging money leaks by shopping at home.

Half-and-half journal   The place where you jot down your thoughts, dollar sign moments, and answers to the journal questions found in this book.

Life clues   Reminder notes you leave for yourself.

Lost and found   A single box, basket, drawer, shelf, or container where you toss other people's belongings that they leave around, so that you can avoid having to put them away.

Maybe box   A box where you store items you are not absolutely sure you can part with. You have one year to decide whether you need each object. On the box's one-year expiration date, if you can name anything that is in the box, you can have it back.

Menu board   A list of leftovers and snacks you have on hand to eat.

Moneyize   = Money + Organize.

Moneyize Group   A group of fellow travelers on the moneyizing journey who gather in person to swap stuff, share tips, and support each other.

NFC   <u>N</u>o <u>F</u>iling <u>C</u>abinet method.

ODS   <u>O</u>rganizing <u>D</u>istraction <u>S</u>yndrome.

One-week rule   You can buy it only if you will put it to use this week.

RICHES   Relate, Identify, Cross-list, Host, Encourage, Scope.

Sellables   Items that you can turn around for cash.

Separation anxiety   Dealing with the feelings that arise when you let an item go.

Shareables   Items you give away without getting anything in exchange.

Shop at home   Look around your home to find items that are suitable to be reused.

Sister-in-law test   If you would not give it to your sister-in-law, don't share it.

Swappables   Items you trade away for something you will use.

Treasure box   A container where you store mementos and treasured items.

Unsellables   Items that you can't sell or use.

How to Get the Most from This Book

I know you have every intention of prioritizing this method of cashing in on your clutter, but I also know you are busy and possibly a tad overwhelmed, right? That's why I wrote this book in an organized and easy-to-digest format. We'll start off discussing the clutter-cash connection, then you'll go room by room and put into place a few low- and no-cost organizing solutions as you clean up while tracking down treasures to sell. Finally, you'll sell the items you found. The best way to read this book is from cover to cover, but if you are under a deadline or prefer to jump in using a thirty-day plan, I've provided one for you in chapter 12.

As you go through the book, you will undoubtedly read things you'll want to remember, so be sure to jot them down. I, for one, can't bring myself to write in a book. If you can, then go for it. If not, attach sticky notes to the pages, but don't forget to write *why* you marked the page. Nothing is worse than referring back to a flagged page and having no clue why you flagged it in the first place.

The Money Saver boxes in each chapter highlight some easy ideas to help you claim the cash that is hidden in the clutter traps throughout your home. In addition, each chapter lists the most common items that will earn you money, so you know where to start looking.

Start a Moneyize Group

Another great way to keep yourself motivated and on track is to locate at least one other person who is on the same page as you, to form a Moneyize Group. I run a monthly Moneyize Group by phone that you are welcome to join, but in-person groups provide something special and I strongly encourage them.

Let's face it, doing this by yourself can get lonely. You can lose momentum after a while if you don't have support and accountability. Sure, you may look to your spouse, but maybe your spouse is not the best source of unconditional understanding in this area. So, you might turn to a family member or a coworker; having someone lend an ear and offer advice can make all the difference. But then life happens and, without having scheduled times to talk with this person, you can once again find yourself alone and struggling. I don't want that to happen to you.

Imagine sitting face-to-face with other people who are also using the half-and-half method. You can scoop up ideas and motivation; you can share tips and successes, as well as your struggles. I'll bet you think this is a great idea, but it also sounds like there is a lot of work involved. You might be panicking a little to think of inviting people over to your home for a meeting.

The good news is that I've done almost all of the work for you. You'll simply use this book as a guide for what to talk about when your Moneyize Group meets. How convenient is that? There are just a few other things you'll need to get started. And the part about inviting people over for a meeting—what better excuse could you have to start cleaning? Seriously, though, if you are not ready for company, you can rotate using the homes of the members, or you could meet in a public location, such as a café, library, a house of worship, or a bookstore.

Here are the steps you can follow to create your own wildly successful Moneyize Group. Once you do, let me know whether you'd like me to mention that you're looking for members. I hope you'll consider inviting me to drop in, either in person, if I'm touring in the area, or by speakerphone. I'd really like to meet you!

Ten Steps to Starting Your Own Moneyize Group

1. Locate at least one other person who struggles with getting everything done, although three to seven members is ideal. Consider your children's classmates' mothers, coworkers, friends, family, neighbors, friends, or acquaintances from your house of worship and other parents from your children's daycare or extracurricular activities.

2. Invite the person or people to be part of the group.

3. Choose a place, a date, and a time to meet. Decide whether the group will meet weekly or monthly.

4. Be sure that everyone takes the CAM quiz and gets his or her CAM score prior to the first meeting.

5. At the first meeting, discuss your quiz results.

6. Consider designating a timekeeper to ensure that everyone has a chance to participate.

7. By the end of the meeting, be sure that each person has stated a goal that he or she plans to have accomplished before the next meeting.

8. Assign the next section of the book to be read before the next meeting.

9. Stay in touch between meetings to give one another support.

10. Check out JamieNovak.com for more updates, printable handouts, and resources.

Take the Self-Assessment Clutter and Money (CAM) Quiz

Before we go much further, I think it's important to take a moment to determine where you are. If you don't know where you are starting from, it is more difficult to know where you are going or to look back to see how far you've come. That's why I created this simple exam. It's a ten-question self-assessment quiz that will help you determine your Clutter and Money (CAM) score. Your CAM score is based on how financially healthy and happy you are today.

CAM scores range from 100 to 500 points, with 250 being average and 500 being excellent. The great news is that you can change your CAM score; even a single small change can make a big difference. No matter where you are starting from, as long as you start, there is hope for a higher score and a richer life. Record your score in your half-and-half journal. Be sure to make a note of the date. You'll retake the quiz at the end of the book and again every three months to check your progress.

Choose the description under each question that most applies to you today, and assign yourself the corresponding point value. Just a quick reminder: now is the time to be completely honest. You have no one to impress and no one to compare yourself to. No one is judging you. We simply need to get an accurate gauge of your current situation so that we can set you on the right course. Ready? Here we go:

1. If guests stopped by unexpectedly, you'd:

    Dive under the table and pretend you weren't home. **10 points**

    Leave them waiting outside while you scooped up clutter from the tabletops. **20 points**

    Meet them on the front porch and avoid inviting them inside. **30 points**

    Run around and close a few doors to untidy rooms before inviting them in. **40 points**

    Open the door and invite them in. **50 points**

2. How often do you arrive late for appointments, even by "just ten minutes"?

    All the time. **10 points**

    Most of the time. **20 points**

    About 50 percent of the time. **30 points**

    Not very often and not without a good reason. **40 points**

    Not ever. In fact, I am usually early. **50 points**

3. Your home office:

    Is so buried it would take an excavation crew to locate it. **10 points**

Is a makeshift space, such as the corner of a dining room table. **20 points**

Looks like a tornado whipped through it. **30 points**

Has a stack of unfiled papers, but other than that, it's good. **40 points**

Has a clean desk and all papers are filed. **50 points**

4. You have to go grocery shopping. You:

Walk out the door and go. **10 points**

Check the pantry to see what you have and what you need before you go. **20 points**

Pick up the list off the counter and go. **30 points**

Add items you need to your list by looking in the pantry and then plan your shopping trip to coincide with other errands you need to run in the area. **40 points**

You log onto the store's delivery service online, add what you need to your cart from the reorder list, and choose a convenient delivery time. **50 points**

5. Do you own *and* regularly use a shredder to dispose of all papers that contain sensitive information?

Yes **40 points**

No **20 points**

6. Loose change in your home is:

Scattered about and under couch cushions. **10 points**

Collected in multiple containers. **30 points**

Deposited in a single container and occasionally taken to the bank. **50 points**

7. Is your important paperwork securely stored in a fireproof box or a safety deposit box?

Yes **40 points**

No **20 points**

8. Do you have an account set up where you regularly deposit sums of money to be used in the event of an unexpected emergency?

Yes **40 points**

No **20 points**

9. Do you know your current checking account balance within twenty dollars?

Yes **40 points**

No **20 points**

10. One night you can't sleep and flip on the television to an infomercial. After watching for a few minutes, you start to think it looks like something you need, and you:

Turn off the television. **50 points**

Pick up the phone and then stop yourself. **30 points**

Call and order it. **10 points**

Add up your points to get your score, then note the date and the score in your half-and-half journal:

1–100 points: Uh-oh, budget buster! The good news is that you can make major improvements with a few small changes. Turn to chapter 1 and start reading.

101–200 points: Whoops, you're not on the right track—yet. But you're trying, and that's the first step. You are on your way to success.

201–300 points: Average savings. Most readers will fall in this range, so you are at a great starting point.

301–400 points: Close to cashing in! Minor tweaks will get you where you want to be. You are doing a lot that's right already. Imagine how much more you'd have if you took it up a notch.

401–500 points: Right on the money, and I'll bet you love learning new tips and ideas. This book is perfect for you. Not only will you read about things you are already doing right, but you'll also discover new and clever ideas.

Are You Broke and Disorganized?

The Clutter-Cash Connection

Disorganization and our bank account balances go hand in hand. Some of the ways are obvious, such as when we misplace bills and accrue late fees or save a box of items for a yard sale that we never hold. Other ways are not as obvious; for example, when we toss away perfectly good shoeboxes and then go out and buy boxes to use as drawer organizers, or we buy another jar of paprika because the original one is lost in the pantry. We've all done it, but with a little organization in our homes and lives, we can do it less often, which will save us more money.

During my years of working with multitudes of clients and giving hundreds of lectures nationwide, I've identified *four* key areas where clutter and cash connect. Which ones can you relate to the most?

1. **We can't find what we own, so we simply buy more.**
   As I said, we've all done it. Admit it, what's the last thing
   you bought, knowing full well that you already had one
   but just couldn't put your finger on where it was? For me,
   it was a gift bag. I set aside a gift bag for an upcoming
   birthday, and I put it in such a special place that I could
   not find it when I needed it. So I shelled out another four
   bucks to buy a new one. Guess when I found the one
   I already had? Yep, when I walked in from the party!
   There it was, sitting on top of the entertainment center,
   right where I'd safely tucked it away. I used to think, Oh,
   it's only four dollars. Now I think, Oh, my gosh, it's four
   dollars!

2. **We hold on to items of sellable value.** The average
   home has about twenty-five items of value going to waste
   that could be sold for a tidy profit. For example:

   - A little black dress that was never worn, with the tags
     still on it, shoved into the back of a closet = $140

   - A DVD movie left out on the floor, stepped on, and
     cracked in two = $14

   - A learn-to-knit box kit, complete with yarn and nee-
     dles, never opened = $14

   - A value pack of printer ink, and you no longer own the
     printer = $50

   - A newly released book from a hot new author, never
     read = $24

   - A takeout container of leftover Chinese food, or at least
     I think it was Chinese food = $10

   Okay, so maybe the leftover Chinese is not sellable, but
   you get the idea. From this sample list, the total wasted in
   one month alone was $252. Now, multiply that by twelve

months and you get a whopping $3,024! Sure, half-and-half organizing worked for my other clients, but can it work for you? Absolutely! In fact, you may save even *more* per year. We'll get to this in detail later on, but I promise you that the solutions are supersimple and budget friendly.

3. **We don't repurpose what we already own, we simply buy new.** Instead of discarding items that are still good, try to find alternative uses for them. Think about this:

- Buy a storage unit for the garage. **$400**
  Use an old dresser. **Free**

- Buy an art-supply caddy. **$20**
  Use a dish drying rack. **Free**

- Buy a plastic shopping bag holder. **$10**
  Use a canvas tote bag. **Free**

- Buy a jewelry organizer for the drawer. **$80**
  Use an egg carton. **Free**

- Buy a drawer organizer for three drawers. **$45**
  Use a variety of box lids. **Free**

I know what you're saying: "Jamie, you're so creative. I could never come up with all of these alternative solutions

MONEY SAVER

Did you know that you can accumulate $10,000 a year by saving only $27.40 a day? That's less than one bounced check fee daily or equal to using pizza boxes instead of buying specialty archival boxes for your children's drawings.

my own." First of all, I don't believe that. Once you start to look at possible uses for an item, other than the one originally intended for it, all sorts of ideas will come to mind. But just in case they don't, because this is such an important topic, I've dedicated an entire chapter to reusing, repurposing, and finding alternative uses for common household items so that you can release your inner crafter.

4. **We allow clutter-cash traps to go unattended.** Raise your hand if you've been putting off doing something that you know has the potential to make or save you money. It could be returning an item to the store or calling to stop the item-of-the-month club membership you no longer want. But you're busy and you put it off. Before you know it, another thirty days have gone by, and you've accrued an additional subscription fee or lost out on the full credit of the return because it is over the time limit or the receipt is missing. Hundreds of dollars can slip through your fingers in this key area, but a few simple fixes will keep that money in your pocket.

The Differences between Wasteful Organizing and Moneyizing

When you organize, you toss out the old, but when you moneyize, you repurpose the old.

When you organize, you make a box of things to sell, but when you moneyize, you actually do sell the things in the box.

When you organize, you store the items that represent your past and your future, but when you moneyize, you get clear about what you want and who you are today.

When you organize, you store collections and memorabilia in a contained way, but when you moneyize, you use it instead of simply letting it collect dust.

When you organize, you purge, then buy more, but when you moneyize, you choose to own less.

When you organize, you allow your belongings to have power over you, but when you moneyize, you take control of your belongings.

When you organize, you resent all of your clutter, but when you moneyize, you have an attitude of gratitude for all that you can afford.

What's *That* Got to Do with Being Organized?

At first glance, you wouldn't think that asking for a good driver discount or calling your credit card company to request a lower interest rate would have much to do with being organized. But, in fact, these tasks have everything to do with organizing. You can make the calls only *if* you can locate the paperwork or have a system to remember to tackle time-saving projects such as comparison shopping, reconciling accounts, and paying more attention to the money-saving details.

If you had a fifty-dollar bill, you wouldn't carelessly let it sit out on a table or stuff it in a drawer. But an unsubmitted rebate for fifty dollars from a recently purchased printer is the same thing. When you start to look at that pile of papers and other items as if they have dollar signs attached to them, they take on a whole new meaning. You are less likely to allow them to collect dust and more likely to take action when there is an opportunity to make or save money.

What Does "Rich" Mean to You?

Each person would define a rich life in his or her own way, and that's how it should be. I think a rich life includes having not only a healthy bank balance and as little debt as possible, but also the time, energy, and ability to connect with those you love. Only *you* know what feels healthy to you and what makes you happy. Of course, there are minimum requirements to meet in order for a person to be considered financially and organizationally fit, but above and beyond that, the rest is up to you.

The basics include:

- Knowing how much you make and spend in a month
- Consistently spending less than you earn
- Automatically saving a percentage of your income
- Having no debt or working on a plan to eliminate debt
- Having your assets protected
- Storing your important financial documents in a disaster-proof container
- Paying your bills on time and being up-to-date with your taxes
- Having a little something set aside to cover the unexpected
- Being able to find what you need when you need it
- Holding on to only those items you use and love
- Setting aside time on a regular basis to de-clutter

Beyond these criteria, I personally think it comes down to comfort and security. When you are comfortable, you feel healthy, and when you are secure, you can feel happy. Half-and-half organizing is the way to a rich life however you would define it.

Where's the Money?

There's really not a single object you can point to and say, "That's it! That's the one that caused my clutter-cash issues."

It's never only one large item or purchase that causes all of the problems. If it were, you'd be able to get rid of it, sell it, or do something so that you could get back on track. You might try to place the blame on a large purchase that revealed itself to be unnecessary, such as a new set of furniture or a shopping spree, but that's not it. Although this purchase probably didn't help, it's not the one that's to blame.

Instead, surprisingly, the problem is the accumulation that results from your daily habits. All of the small, seemingly insignificant choices you make on a daily basis get you to where you are. It's shocking, I know. It seems much more likely that a few extravagant purchases would be to blame, but no, it's the little stuff. Want to see what I mean? Grab a calculator or a pen and paper, or, if you're a math whiz and can add numbers in your head without losing track, you can skip using these tools. Personally, I can barely add two numbers in my head without messing up, but do whatever works for you.

Now walk over to your media collection: CDs, DVDs, and video games. Take a quick glance: which ones haven't been used in the last six months? Be honest, I know that at least one has a layer of dust on it. How much did it cost? Add up the approximate cost of all the ones that have gone unused. Are there one or two that never even made it out of that annoyingly difficult to open plastic wrapper? Try not to feel guilty. Simply add them to your total, and let's move on.

Now head over to your bookshelf. Which books did you buy but have not read yet? Add those to the list as well. It's not only the media items and the books; it's the clothes, the collections, and the other clutter. So, what's your total so far: $20, $60, maybe even $100?

We'll look at one more key area before I let you off the hook. Take a walk into your kitchen, one of the biggest money pits of all. I've dedicated an entire chapter to the kitchen later in the book, where I've cooked up some quick fixes to share with you.

Swing open the pantry door, and add up the approximate cost of all the things you have bought and not used. The bottle of fish sauce you bought when you thought you might learn to make fried rice, the package of seasoning that you don't even remember buying. You're not on *The Price Is Right*, so just estimate what the items cost and add them up.

Finally, let's hit the fridge. Take a look inside, and add up the cost of the food you will have to throw away. Maybe a half-gallon of milk past its date, a spoiled veggie or two, or perhaps an icky container of something that's so old, you don't know what it used to be.

What's your total now: $80, $120, or more? Now take that number and multiply it by 12 for the twelve months of the year. In these few areas of your home, let's pretend that you just found $100. Multiplied by 12, that's $1,200, which could be in your pocket instead of cluttering up your home.

I'm not asking you to do this to make you feel bad—honest. It's just that when you use your own personal items in the equation, it becomes much more real. So, look around you. That's where the money is. Now it is your job to recapture that money and put your clutter to work for you. To do that, let's look at how we justify the clutter-cash issue.

Lies We Tell Ourselves

Have you ever made any of the following comments? If you have, you're not alone. These are the most popular reasons why we tend to hold on to something. Call them excuses, reasons, justifications, or whatever; true or not, they are what we tell ourselves to avoid accountability. Now, every other organizer I know would have a clever comeback and would offer cliché

advice. But you already know that I'm not like every other organizer. I've put my own spin on a few old misconceptions, and
you may be surprised to hear what I have to say. So go ahead,
give me your best reason, and I'll show you why you're *right*!

The lie: "It'll come in handy one day."

What most people will tell you: Throw it away today;
holding on to an item just in case sometime in the future you
might need it creates clutter. There is no way you'll remember that you have it when you need it, and you'll only buy
another one anyway.

Why that's wrong: Throwing away gently used or new
items is like throwing away money. They add to our over-
crowded landfills and rob you of a chance to sell them or
share them with someone who can put them to good use.

The lie: "It's still good."

What most people will tell you: Let it go. It may be good,
but it's no good to you.

Why that's wrong: If you can use those margarine containers and the cardboard tubes from the rolls of paper towels,
go right ahead. Not having to buy a stack of small containers can save you up to $10. Do that once a month, and that's
$120 you've saved in a year.

The lie: "But I might need it."

What most people will tell you: If you have not used it in
a year, you should throw it out.

Why that's wrong: You're right. You might need it, so
forgo the arbitrary one-year rule and designate a single place
to store a handful of items you may use one day. That way,
you'll have them when you need them and will not have to
rebuy them.

The lie: "I love it."

What most people will tell you: If it is so useful, why is it buried in the closet?

Why that's wrong: If you love it, use it or display it. If you foresee being able to use it in the near future, store it away properly—and in such a way that you'll remember you have it. We're human; we can forget that we own something. Or, it could be that our tastes or our circumstances have changed, and now we have the space and the opportunity to use that item.

The lie: "I have to keep this, it reminds me of . . ."

What most people will tell you: The memory is not in the item; it is in your head. You don't need to keep the actual object because you'll always have the memory.

Why that's wrong: Although it is true that the memory is not inside the actual item, seeing the item is the trigger that brings back the fond memory, so we do need to have certain items around. Taking and keeping a picture of the item can sometimes be all that you need to jog your memory. You can also keep part of the item; for example, if you have a broken chair with a needle-crafted seat by your great-grandmother, let the broken chair go and frame the needle-crafted seat.

The lie: "One day I'll get to this."

What most people will tell you: You are living for the future. You may have grand plans of how you will spend your time when you have more of it. So you hold on to all sorts of items, thinking, One day I'll . . . Instead of keeping the stuff, let someone else use it now.

Why that's wrong: It is impossible to predict when you'll have a free moment to get to a project or when inspiration will strike and you'll want to start something you've been putting off. If you don't have the supplies you need, you won't be able to begin the project. Keep a running list of the items you have so that when you make time to do the projects, you can get the stuff you need. Think about where you are today in your life, your interests, and the amount of time and space you have to start a project. Then, choose the top few projects accordingly.

The lie: "It was on sale."

What most people will tell you: Stocking up on something because it is a bargain or purchasing misfit clothing because you "could probably wear this someday" is not a deal by any stretch of the imagination. Practice passing up so-called sales.

Why that's wrong: Who doesn't love to save money with a good bargain? Stock up on what you need when you can get a good deal; just don't overrun the amount of storage space you have. And always shop from a list to avoid impulsive and unnecessary purchases.

The lie: "It was free."

What most people will tell you: If it's a pen from your doctor's office or a mug from the bank—unless you need another pen or mug—it will take up space, forcing you to clean around it while you provide free advertising!

Why that's wrong: If you simply think of a mug as a mug, then that's true. Do you really need another one? Probably not; however, using a mug as a Q-tip holder in the bathroom or a penholder in the office or even a paintbrush holder in your craft area is cost-effective storage. If you can think of an alternative use for an item, go for it. You'll save yourself money in the process.

The lie: "I paid good money."

What most people will tell you: No matter what you paid for it, if you keep it but don't use it, it is still a waste. Resolve yourself to the fact that you did not make the best purchase decision, and let the item go to someone who will love and use it.

Why that's wrong: An item you never used can be sold for more than a gently used item can. Make all or at least some of your money back so that you don't feel as bad for not using the item. Make time to sell the item, and, in the future, either use items or return them, so that you don't lose the money you spent.

The lie: "I like being prepared."

What most people will tell you: Sometimes what we learned while growing up sticks with us as adults. One example is the fear of not having enough because of a real time when there was not enough, such as during the Depression. If you were taught to be thrifty and to reuse or hold on to things out of fear, then you may be repeating those habits today.

Why that's wrong: With finances the way they are today, there is a real possibility of not having enough. Either way, why discard something that is useful? Tell yourself that you will always be taken care of. This will help calm any anxiety you may feel that is based on old fears. If you reuse good items and continue to save money by becoming even more organized, you will ensure that you'll have enough for the future.

Small Changes *Can* Make a Big Difference

If getting your finances organized were as simple as paying your bills on time to avoid racking up costly late fees, there would not be much to talk about, would there? Sure, knowing where your unpaid bills are so that you can pay them before the due date is important. But let's be honest—who hasn't heard that overused advice? It's not as if you set out to pay our bills late. Sometimes it simply happens, usually because the bill was misplaced and forgotten. So, yes, it makes sense to have a place to stash the bills so that you remember to pay them on time. Later in the book, I will describe some simple ways to organize key areas of your life that will make a financial difference.

Yet these crucial tasks, such as bill paying, don't tell the whole story. There are so many ways that clutter costs us, and it is the smaller, much less obvious ways that actually are the worst. Does it help to pay your bills on time? You bet. But you can do so much more that can pay off in a big way.

MARYANN'S STORY

Maryann represents a cautionary tale. She called me on a Monday, after yet another weekend of arguing with her husband about how much their disorganization was costing them. As she spoke, I filled out my new client form. She was married, the mother of two teenage boys, with a prominent job in the community. Her husband was a respected physician in town, and, like most of us, they were superbusy.

Maryann admitted that the last straw was when her oldest son came to her that night before bed and said, "If it will help, I'll sell my video games because they take up space in the living room."

After comparing calendars, we set a date for our first session, and I asked for her home address. There was an awkward silence on the other end of the line, and I wondered whether she was rethinking her decision to get started. But as it turned out, that was not the reason for her pause.

Maryann told me she was not sure which address to give me. I explained that we'd start at her home and move on to her office or vacation home if we needed to. "No, you don't understand," she said. "I don't know which home address to give you." She admitted that they owned three homes. The first two were so full of clutter, they were uninhabitable. I reminded her that as an organizer, I make no judgments. I told her that the policy is not for her to tidy up before I arrive, because I need to see items in their natural state. "Don't worry," she joked. "I couldn't tidy up even if I tried."

Our first session was a huge success. As we organized her entryway, she told me about how they came to be paying for three homes but were able to live in only one. It started, she thought, with the birth of their first child. She said that their once superorganized home began to show signs of disorganization: lost car keys, piles of mail, missed bill payments. It escalated with each career promotion, new baby, and stressful life event, such as the death of her mother. She said it got even worse when her husband, Ted, won his first online auction. Maryann said that from then on, he spent an increasing number of hours online, bidding on items.

I asked what he was bidding on, and she showed me. Stacked floor to ceiling in a spare bedroom, with just enough room to barely open the door, were shoes, men's shoes of all styles and colors. "Does he wear any of these?" I asked. "No," she said. "In fact, many are not even his size." Most of the shoes were still in their original packaging, and some had not even been taken out of their shipping boxes.

Getting down to work, Maryann showed me what she and the two previous organizers had attempted. They'd tossed out a dresser and box after box, then they'd shopped for her and returned from the organizing store with new boxes and a chest of drawers. This approach was illogical, because they purchased items that were similar to the ones they had thrown away. They hadn't even sold or given away the boxes and drawers; they had merely tossed them into a landfill. This cost Maryann precious time and money that she did not have, especially with three mortgages to pay.

As a team, Maryann and Ted worked with me, and we made real progress. With so much reclaimed space, time, and energy, Maryann and Ted reconnected and realigned their GPS. In other words, they got their priorities straight. Instead of valuing objects, they cherished their time spent as a family, which meant that Ted stopped buying shoes.

Their oldest son did not have to sell his video games. It took slightly longer than eighteen months of their working together, but they are down to one home and a single large storage unit. And all of those shoes? Some were given away to men who needed shoes for job interviews; the rest were sold for a whopping grand total of more than $23,000!

Along with recovering their bank balance, Maryann and Ted revived their marriage and now have a full and rich life.

Maryann's story is a bit extreme, but it can happen. That small pile of mail can turn into a mountain, and those collectibles can soon require a room of their own, costing you lots of money and so much more.

Ways We Avoid Organizing

When we say: It has to be perfect.

What we really mean is: I'll never be able to live up to the impossible standard I set for myself, so why try?

When we say: I don't know where to start.

What we really mean is: I'm too overwhelmed.

When we say: I'll get to it later.

What we really mean is: I'm too lazy to make a decision right now.

When we say: Why bother? It won't make that much difference.

What we really mean is: It's too far gone; a small change won't help.

When we say: I don't have the time.

What we really mean is: I'm not going to make the time. This is not a priority for me.

Aside from Money, What Is Clutter Costing You?

Sure, it seems innocent enough—the stuffed bear or the decorative basket that makes its way into your home. At first glance, you'd never guess items like these are costing you a fortune. And I don't mean the money you spent to buy them. The problem is so much bigger than that.

I call it the clutter quotient: what an item really costs to buy, own, care for, store, and clean around, then dispose of.

Aside from the dollar figure, clutter affects you in other ways, one of which is your happiness. It's true. Just think back to the last time you arrived home in a good mood, only to open the front door to see a mound of shoes, a stack of mail, and a pile of things to deal with later. How long did your good mood last? How happy were you then?

These are the ways that clutter can take a toll on our lives, financially and otherwise.

- In your relationships, you can second-guess yourself and your ability to be a good role model if you're disorganized. You can aggravate people around you with your chronic lateness. Your self-esteem can be diminished if you feel unsuccessful because you can't organize your life. Arguments with family members and loved ones over the clutter can take their toll. Clutter acts as a barrier to your closeness with a partner; it's difficult to feel harmonious when you can't see the bed beneath the mess. And if you've stopped entertaining because of the chaos in your house, then you're missing out on creating memories with people you care about.

- Clutter drains your energy, and you won't realize it until that energy is already gone. Even your health can suffer because of the mess. Clutter can make it more difficult to eat healthy foods because you can't cook in a disorganized kitchen. Your home might not be as clean or as dust- and allergen-free when you're disorganized—not to mention the fact that piles of objects are hazards that you may trip and fall over.

- Regarding your career, you might be passed over for a promotion because you always miss deadlines, or you might receive a poor performance review due to a messy desk. You might even miss out on job opportunities because you misplace a key contact's information or forget about an interview appointment.

Get into the Habit of Organizing

You can resist your urge to simply buy something new, stop at a yard sale, or put the mail on the kitchen counter to sort through later. Whether you actually do resist is another story. Organization is a habit, plain and simple. You do not need any special degrees or skills, and contrary to popular belief, you do not need to be born organized to maintain an organized lifestyle. You can learn the habits, starting today. When you walk in the door, toss your receipts in a single location, so that you'll be able to find them if you need to return an item or compare them with an incoming statement.

Busy versus Lazy

I hate to bring this up, but if we're going to be honest, it needs to be put out there. Laziness plays a big part in the clutter-cash connection. I once worked with a client who showed me a camera bag full of memory cards. Instead of simply reading about how to download the digital pictures onto her computer, she kept buying more memory cards. Here are a few ways that being lazy might affect your bottom line:

- Is my shirt stained? I'm too lazy to clean it, so I'll simply get a new one.

- I can't find the printer cartridge I bought. I'm too lazy to look for it, so I'll buy a new one.

- No socks? I'm too lazy to put in a load of laundry, so I'll just buy more socks.

- I'm too lazy to think outside the box, so I'll skip reusing a perfectly good item.

Let's not confuse *busy* with *lazy*. *Busy* is the term we often use when we're really just too lazy. We could make the time, but most often, we simply choose not to. Yet if getting organized and saving money are truly priorities, then none of these excuses will fly.

Now that you can clearly see the connection between clutter and money, it's time to put the principles behind half-and-half organizing into action. You're going to focus your efforts and accomplish something you can really be proud of.

Stop Procrastinating and Organize Your Life

Embracing Your To-Do List

During the many years that I've been helping people save money by getting organized, I've noticed something. Just because we know what we *should* be doing does not mean we're actually doing it. We know that using half-and-half organizing to de-clutter our lives would be good for our pocketbooks and for ourselves, but we put off getting started. Here's why:

- We're out of time and energy so we can't get started.
- We're overwhelmed and simply not sure what to do first.
- We want to do it right, perfect even, and fear making a mistake.
- We are uncomfortable making decisions about what to keep and what to toss.
- We are not faced with a deadline and have no one to hold us accountable.

Do You Suffer from ODS (Organizing Distraction Syndrome)?

When was the last time you experienced ODS (organizing distraction syndrome)? It goes something like this:

> You start a project: Let's say you set out to clear your bedside table. It seems like a simple enough organizing task that will take only a few minutes. You start with the overflowing stack of magazines. While sorting them into "recycle" and "to read" piles, you flip one open and see an article about a Web site with advice on how to stop junk mail. You don't want to forget to visit this useful site, so you decide you'd better do it now. After all, it will take only a minute.
>
> You hop on the computer and look up the site. Then, since you're on the computer anyway, you take an extra minute to check your e-mail. While you're reading a joke-of-the-day e-mail, the phone rings. It's your neighbor, asking you to pet sit. You can't think of a good excuse fast enough, so now you are on the hook. You get up to write the dates on your calendar, and while you're in the kitchen, you start a load of dishes. You notice that it is time for dinner, so you grab a snack. By now, you've been in every room of the house, but the bedside table still looks the same or maybe even worse.

You have a clear case of ODS: starting an organizing project but getting distracted before you can finish it. The prescription? Before you begin your task, set a timer for eighteen minutes. The rule is, you can't leave that area or start another task until the buzzer goes off. You must make a list of anything that is off topic so that you can handle it later. And if you find items that belong in another part of the house, make a pile and deliver them to the appropriate spot after time is up.

Finding More Time

Let's get real; there are only twenty-four hours in the day, and we're already very busy. Sometimes the added pressure of finding time to clean up and create a rich life can send us over the edge. We repeatedly tell other people how busy we are. In fact, sometimes we get into "busy contests." Think about what happens when you run into someone you haven't seen in a while. When she asks how you are, you say, "Oh, I've been busy." Then she feels obligated to explain that she's been busy, too. It can turn into a competition about who's been the busiest, who has the most going on, and who has the most demands on her time. Let's agree that we're all busy, but one thing I know for sure is that if you *really* want to do something, you'll make the time. Creating a rich life does not happen in your spare time, if there even is such a thing. The only way that you'll have time for something is when you set time aside. Don't wait to find it accidentally because this will never happen.

Maybe you're like most people and you're waiting for a *whole day* to get organized. I can certainly understand your not wanting to start a project that you won't have time to finish. So you plan on tackling a task when you have a large block of time to work on it, maybe six or eight hours that you can dedicate to a single project. The problem is, I don't know anyone who has six or eight uninterrupted hours. And let's be honest, if you did, would you *really* want to organize? I don't think so!

But let's just say that you *did* have an entire Saturday free, and you have every intention of getting around to de-cluttering your pantry area. Your Saturday might go something like this. Because it's Saturday, you sleep in a little. By the time you get moving, it's midmorning and you still need to have a bite to eat before you start. But there's no sense in your making breakfast and then having a mess to clean up in the kitchen before you can even begin to organize the pantry. So you step out to grab a little something to eat. Since you're already out, you pop into the bank. While at the bank, you run into your daughter's friend's mother, who asks whether you are ready for school spirit day on Monday. You say yes, but inside you cringe, knowing you are so *not* ready. As soon as you get home, you hunt down your daughter's school logo T-shirt and pop it into the washing machine. But there's no sense in washing only one T-shirt; you might as well put in a full load. By now, your stomach is growling because it's nearing lunchtime. No worries, you still have the whole afternoon to organize the pantry. So you make lunch, clean up, fold the laundry, check your e-mail, make a phone call, and bring in the mail. When you look at the clock, you realize you've been busy all day but have not touched the pantry. Yet now you're too tired and don't have enough time to start the project after all. It is almost dinnertime, and you have been sidetracked by ODS once again.

First, take the pressure off by telling yourself you have plenty of time. Whenever you feel the busiest, repeat out loud, "I have more than enough time to create an organized and rich life."

The good news is that you do not need as much time as you think. In fact, we tend to grossly overestimate how long organizing projects will take. You can stop waiting for big blocks of time when you don't need them. Success happens when you take small, consistent steps. I highly recommend my brownie mix method, which consists of organizing in eighteen-minute blocks of time, the same amount of time it would take to bake a batch of gooey brownies. Why eighteen? Well, ten is too short to get anything done, and twenty feels too long. I know you're thinking that at only eighteen minutes a shot, it could take you eighty-two years to get organized. Not true. You can get *a lot* done in just eighteen minutes of focused time. Surprisingly, eighteen minutes of uninterrupted time is as good as fifty minutes of multitasking. Granted, some projects simply make more sense to do as a marathon session, but use caution. Unless you have a team of helpers, you might pull all of the items out that you need to organize and not have enough time to finish. For each area you work on, choose which method will work best, based on how much time you have, how much help (if any) you have, and how quickly you want results. And if you don't have a lot of time right now, don't wait for more free time to come along in some ideal future scenario. That won't happen. Instead, try the eighteen-minute brownie mix method to get started.

Creating More Energy

Aside from time, you need energy, both physical *and* mental, to be able to do the work. Honestly, sometimes you're simply too tired, stressed out, or down in the dumps to feel motivated to take action. We've all been there. We know we should tackle a certain project, and maybe we even really want to do it, but we simply feel unable to put one foot in front of the other. I won't sugarcoat it because there is a certain amount of effort involved in accomplishing any task. Some of it is mental, such as making decisions, and other efforts are physical, like moving items, possibly up and down stairs, bagging up certain things, and moving objects, sometimes even furniture.

So, how can you muster up the necessary energy? First, you need to deal with the mental clutter, and by this, I mean everything you have rolling around in your head, all of the details you are trying to remember about what to do and buy, whom to call, and even what to make for dinner. You try to remember too much, and when your brain is full, you can have trouble falling or staying asleep. This exhausting cycle leaves you physically tired.

De-clutter your mind by getting out your half-and-half journal, then write down anything and everything that you are thinking. Forget spelling, grammar, and penmanship; simply write. The idea is to get these thoughts out of your head and onto the paper. Your journal might turn into a to-do list of sorts, or it might not. Don't worry about organizing your thoughts in any particular way. The key is to de-clutter your mind. You may need to repeat this process every so often, so that you can start with a clean slate.

Once you've wiped away the mental clutter, you will be more clearheaded and able to sleep and focus better. Being well rested *automatically* gives you more energy. Be sure to eat well. Candy bars and cookies are good for a short burst of sugar-induced energy, but you'll end up napping on the pile of papers you're supposed to be sorting if you're not careful. Instead, try a sandwich on whole-wheat bread or a banana to keep your energy at a steadier level. And the very best trick I know to boost energy levels is simply to start moving. Movement feeds energy, and if you can trick yourself into thinking you have enough energy to start, then you'll be able to finish. I know it sounds odd, but it works, trust me.

Fifteen Ways to (Finally) Achieve Your Goals

Who hasn't procrastinated about doing something, at one time or another? Perhaps it was an unpleasant task, such as making a dentist's appointment or filing a stack of bills, not knowing which ones to keep and which to shred. Maybe we needed to locate a receipt before we could return an item to a store. Or we had planned to send a well-deserved but now long overdue thank-you note. Sometimes we have put things off until they became emergencies or too overwhelming to handle. Well, no more! It's time for you to find your personal procrastination solution, a technique that will work for you whenever you need it. Stop putting things off and take control, by using one of the following fifteen tips:

1. **Set a timer.** The task as a whole may be overwhelming, but what if you break it up? Don't feel as if you have to do it all or there's no point in doing anything. Instead, set a timer for five minutes, and do a small piece of the project. It's better to accomplish something than nothing, and getting started is the hardest part.

2. **Tell someone (even me).** Have you ever noticed that you are more likely to do something for someone else before you'll do it for yourself? You can make this work for you. Tell someone you trust what you plan to do, and then you'll have to do it because the other person is waiting for you to report back.

3. **Get rewarded.** What if you knew that as soon as your task was complete, you got a treat? Rewards can be a great motivator. Your reward can be something as simple as curling up with a good book, having a long phone conversation with a good friend, or taking a relaxing nap, whatever works for you. (And no, shopping is not a reward.)

4. **Buddy up.** Someone you know is also procrastinating about something. You can buddy up with this person and motivate each other to get the tasks accomplished.

5. **Dream big.** Instead of thinking about how much you are not looking forward to a task, imagine what it will be like to have it finished and behind you. Sometimes simply focusing on the feeling of being done is enough to get yourself started.

6. **Be guilt free.** Are you embarrassed about something? Do you feel guilty? Should you have done it sooner? Did you wait too long? Do it anyway. Send that birthday card with a short belated note, or return that overdue library book. Wouldn't you rather someone mailed you a thank-you note six months late than not at all?

7. **Create a deadline.** Often, you can put off a task because it has no true deadline. Maybe you've been meaning to clear out the basement, which you can do any time, so you procrastinate about getting started. If you get together with your neighbor and plan a yard sale to get rid of the unwanted items that are now piled up in your basement, you'll have a deadline to meet.

8. **Worst first.** When faced with a few tasks, choose the least appealing and do it, so that in comparison, the others will seem easy. Or start with the easiest one to get the ball rolling.

9. **Brainstorm.** Jot down a simple list of reasons why you want to do a task or list the consequences (such as what it is costing you) if you continue to procrastinate. Or try coming up with different ways to get the task done, even if you have to research alternatives.

10. **Swap now.** Do you know someone who actually enjoys the task you've been putting off? If so, let him or her do it, and you can take on doing something that you enjoy for that person. Sometimes swapping a task is not an option, but you might be able to delegate it or hire it out. Yes, you'll have to pay to get it done, but it just might be worth it.

11. **Make it easy.** Sometimes we tend to overcomplicate matters, making them more difficult than they actually are. For example, do you put off shredding sensitive papers?

Where is the shredder located? If you have to dig it out of a closet to use it, then no wonder you wait. Make a task easy, and you just might get it done.

12. **Two minutes.** Try working on the task for only two minutes. You'll either get a little done and stop, or will get so involved that you will keep going. Either way, you win.

13. **Forget perfect.** Instead of holding yourself to an impossible standard and trying to do a task perfectly the first time around, think of it as a rough draft. Just do something. You can always perfect it later.

14. **Make it interesting.** What can you do to make the task fun? Play music, turn it into a game, or change your attitude and choose to stop seeing the task as a dreaded chore.

15. **Make a decision.** You can change your mind, stop fearing that you'll make the wrong choice, and just take action. Are you still unsure? Research the answer, and make a choice. Stop putting things off until later, because, as we know too well, later never comes.

In your half-and-half journal jot down a task you've been putting off for another time. Now write three reasons why you've procrastinated. Next, write three actions you could take to remedy the situation. This will be just what you need to break through the procrastination.

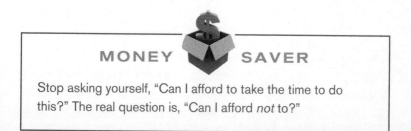

MONEY   SAVER

Stop asking yourself, "Can I afford to take the time to do this?" The real question is, "Can I afford *not* to?"

Organization Is a Lifestyle, *Not* a Destination

Organization is a way of life. You will practice your new routine and new organizing habits every day; this is not something you will complete once and then abandon for the rest of time. Think about the last time you said, "I'll do that *once* I'm finished organizing." You put things off until some mythical future date when you are totally organized; the trouble is, you'll *never* be done. The key is to have a system to deal with your stuff, because the stuff just keeps coming. Even as you sort today's mail pile, tomorrow's mail is already on its way to you. More of everything in life keeps coming; you will buy more shoes and get another bottle of shampoo. The difference is in having a *system*. Your goals and the people living in your home may change over time, but organizational habits will stay with you. Stop waiting!

You might want to join a book club, but you don't do it because you know that the group meetings rotate to all of the members' homes. Eventually, it will be your turn to host the club, and you'd feel uncomfortable inviting guests in until you get the media center organized. The trouble with this continual striving for perfection is that there will always be something to prevent you from living your life fully. The inbox of life is never empty. All of the stuff you're doing is life, while you are waiting for life to start, waiting to join the book club. Just join, and get out there. In fact, knowing that the book club is coming in a few weeks will be all the motivation you need to finally tackle that project and save yourself money. This is a new lifestyle to adopt, not a single change that you need to make. You have a choice each and every day about how organized you'll be. Start today and then take the next step and the next. Small, consistent steps are the keys to lasting success.

Doing Nothing Is Not an Option

Feeling anxious about organizing is a direct result of inaction. Want to feel better instantly? Do something! Creating a richer life by clearing clutter requires action. Stop planning, plotting, and researching; simply use this book as your guide to learn which action to take. If you don't do anything, then you'll get the same broken life you currently have, and we agree that you want more—right? To get that life, you have to *do something*. So, what's your next move? One move leads to the next one, which leads to the next, and so on. Even if you are not sure which move to make, the steps will reveal themselves as you go. Trust the half-and-half process.

Start simple. In the time it takes you to brew a pot of coffee or brush your teeth, you can put money back into your pocket. Just think, if you didn't misplace your house keys and spend fifteen minutes searching for them, or spend ten minutes watching online clips from *Britain's Got Talent* over and over again, you could save big bucks. Start today and you can see instant dividends. Imagine, by this time next month, you could have two hundred more dollars in your bank account. Ka-ching.

Here are ten ten-minute tasks to get you started down the road to a clutter-free lifestyle.

1. **Stop paying late fees for movie rentals.** You forgot to return the last DVD you rented, so you racked up considerable late fees. Sign up with Netflix. Create your personalized queue of films you want to rent on the Netflix site. Netflix will send them to you one at a time (or several at a time, depending upon your subscription level). Keep the movies as long as you want, and then return them in the postage-paid envelope. Never pay a late fee again.

2. **Don't let your cash dry up.** Make a few small changes to your laundry-drying routine, and yield big results.

Toss a clean tennis ball into the dryer, along with a fluffy dry bath towel. The tennis ball will help move the clothes around, and the towel will soak up excess water, thus speeding up the drying process. When you have more than one load to dry, put the next one in before the dryer cools off. Finally, set the dryer to auto off and set a timer as a reminder to get the clothes out before the dryer stops and they wrinkle.

3. **Clean up!** Don't let your dirty laundry soak up your money. Switching your water consumption to cold will save an average of $100 a year on your hot water bill. As an added bonus, it will keep your clothes from fading and shrinking. Replacing your clothes can be very expensive. You might also try adding a cup of white vinegar to the rinse cycle for a full load instead of fabric softener. It sounds odd, but it does work. Don't worry, your clothes will not smell like vinegar.

4. **Courtesy waive.** Annual fees, no thanks. If your credit card company or bank charges an annual fee for the privilege of keeping your money with them, stop! You can move to a no-fee account, or, after the fee is assessed, call the customer service department and ask for the fee to be waived as a courtesy to you, a loyal customer.

5. **Clip your cash.** Ask which of your common retailers accept competitors' coupons and whether they accept these past their expiration dates. You may be surprised that some retailers do.

6. **Give thanks.** Grab a product that you like—shampoo, a frozen dinner, cereal, anything at all—and call the customer service 800 number shown on the package. Let the representative know that you love the product and you plan to remain a loyal customer. For your positive comments, the manufacturer will usually offer you product coupons

and sometimes a certificate for a free product, which is definitely worth a two-minute call. A great side bonus is that customer service reps are so used to receiving negative complaint calls that a positive comment will often brighten his or her workday.

Of course, if for *any reason* you were not 100 percent satisfied, let the company know, and the rep will offer a free replacement. In fact, just last week I called for a replacement certificate for a new flavor of cereal snack; the original one was way too cheesy for my taste.

7. **Gift yourself.** You undoubtedly have at least one gift card or store credit lying around somewhere, waiting to be used. Dig it out right now, place it in your wallet, *and* leave yourself a reminder note to stop at the store or shop online with the coupon during the next week. If you don't need to purchase anything for yourself at the moment, look ahead on the calendar to see what occasions are coming up so that you can buy something for a loved one's birthday, a holiday, or another special event.

8. **Print money (well, almost).** Change the setting on your computer's printer to "fast draft," which is a heck of a lot faster and uses much less ink. When you print something that is superimportant, such as a photo, you can switch back to the regular print setting. But until you get to the very end of the print cartridge, chances are you won't even be able to notice the difference—in the quality, that is. You will certainly notice that you are replacing the cartridges a lot less often. And when you do get to the end of the cartridge, try shaking it to get five to ten more printed sheets from it before you let it go. You can also turn off those printer ink level alerts. Most of the time, they are misleading, which means that you'd replace the ink when the cartridge is still at least a quarter full.

9. **Uncover hidden treasure.** Look under the couch cushion; there's often money hiding under it. Collect loose change in a single place; the most practical spot is near the front door, where you can dump it on your way into the house. When the container is full, don't waste your time rolling it into wrappers. There are places you can go to cash in your change without having to waste hours putting the coins into wrappers. Take your coins to the bank, and deposit the cash! Now, instead of sucking your money into the vacuum cleaner or letting it sit in stacks on the dresser, you can put it to good use.

10. **Cut into your savings.** You know how you can *never* squeeze the very last drop out of the tube of lotion or the toothpaste? What if you cut the package open? You'd have at least one more use out of it, maybe even more. Use the product up completely before you recycle the package. Sure, it might mean breaking it open or getting out the scissors, but it's worth it. Place a pair of good scissors in the bathroom where you'll have to cut open containers. Oh, and another trick to make your money go further is to add water to supplies such as soft soap or dish detergent. You can even add water to mouthwash to double your money. Most of the time, these products are so concentrated you won't notice the difference.

For most organizing projects, you are not faced with a deadline or anyone to hold you accountable. The truth is, it doesn't really matter if you sort your shoes or purge your pantry today or a month from today. You know that the sooner you do it, the more money you'll save, but it can be difficult to get motivated to do the job because no one will be checking on your progress (or lack thereof). The very best way to fit organizing into your schedule and make this happen is to mark it on your calendar.

So, pull out your calendar and think of the next task you want to accomplish, maybe rearranging the fridge or cleaning out your car. Once you know what you'll be working on, mark off the time to do it. Start by setting a deadline. Maybe you want to have it done in three weeks, so mark the finish date on your calendar. Then work backward, blocking off eighteen minutes before your favorite television program is due to air or two hours on the weekend, until you have allocated enough time to finish the project.

Unless you set aside the time, life happens and you won't have any leftover time to dedicate to organizing. Are you thinking that this sounds like a great idea, but you know yourself and expect that despite the time marked on the calendar you will put off the task? If so, then here's what you can do: hold yourself accountable by making a promise that you will keep. For example, if you plan to clean out your closets, call a local charity and make an appointment on a certain date, either for the charity to pick up the unwanted items you'll find in your closets or for you to drop off these items. Once you have a deadline, you'll have to make it happen. In addition, joining a Moneyize Group will keep you on track. I'd love to have you join the monthly Moneyize Group I run over the phone. You can get all the details on my Web site.

Calculate Your Clutter Savings

Hunt for Treasure at Home

How much money would you like to make from your clutter? I know it would be wonderful to sell a childhood baseball card or an heirloom ring for a million dollars, but the chances of that are slim. You can, however, find hundreds or even thousands of dollars under all of that clutter.

So, how much are you looking to bank? Did a specific number come to mind? If so, jot it down in your half-and-half journal. Then think of your goals and work backward to come up with your goal number.

The most popular goals have something to do with:

- Home or car repairs or upgrades
- Lifestyle goals, such as a vacation
- Goals for your children, such as college or a wedding
- Debt elimination or more financial security

Set a realistic monetary goal, and on the inside cover of your half-and-half journal, draw a money goal meter so that you can chart your progress as you go along. Now attach a completion date to your figure. Don't use something generic like "one month" or "one year." Instead, base your goal date on something more meaningful, such as "by my birthday" or "by the beginning of summer." When you divide the amount of money you are looking to make by the number of weeks before your end date, you will determine what you need to accomplish weekly to meet your goal. Write this figure down next to your goal meter for reference.

Are You Living out of a Laundry Basket?

Are your freshly laundered, folded clothes trapped in the laundry basket because there is simply no room in your dressers and closets to put them away? I call this "living out of a laundry basket," and it doesn't only happen with clothes. Throughout your house, the items you use all the time, such as your favorite pair of jeans, can't be put away because the space in your closets and bureaus is taken up by things you used in the past and stuff you might need in the future. This leaves little to no room for anything you use today.

Here are some examples of items from your past that are cluttering up your storage space: the souvenir from your last vacation that sat around for a few months until you got tired of dusting it; the pair of jeans that used to fit but is now a size or three too small, the sheet set for a mattress size that you no longer own, and the ice cream maker from one summer when you were on a homemade ice cream kick. All of these items from your past have dollar signs attached to them.

The trouble with possessions from your past is that they make you feel icky. Seeing those mementos of past vacations reminds you that you haven't gone on a vacation recently, making you feel exhausted and ready for a break. Not to mention the extra time you must spend cleaning around the objects you brought back from that vacation. And seeing those too-small jeans, which used to fit perfectly, makes you feel not good enough and not thin enough. You end up nagging yourself to be thinner or healthier or a different weight or body type. Having those skinny jeans around makes it impossible for you to accept your body as it is, because you have a constant reminder of what you are not. And that ice cream maker might have been useful if it had ever made it out of the box; instead it's another reminder of money you wasted on something you never used—providing yet another blow to your self-esteem.

But the trouble is not only with items from your past; objects you've accumulated for your future are also a problem. For instance, the knitting supplies you picked up when the craft store had a going-out-of-business sale, even though you have no idea how to knit—but you are all set if you ever learn. How about the dress you bought on a whim from the clearance rack that still has the tag on it, hanging in the back of your closet? It's not really your style or color, but it was a good price, and you thought you might find a place to wear it. And let's not even talk about the large plastic bin you picked up to "get organized," which is now sitting in the corner gathering dust. All of this stuff that you might use in the future is, in the meantime, taking up valuable space in your home and making you feel bad every time you see it.

In the meantime someone right in your own town wants to make ice cream but does not have an ice cream maker; someone else needs a dress like the one you never wore; and another person could use the yarn and the needles to knit a baby blanket for a homeless child. And these people are willing to pay you good money for the opportunity.

How Much Can You Earn from Your Clutter?

Are you seeing dollar signs everywhere you look? How much more money would you have if you owned less stuff? And how much money can you make selling your possessions? Let's take an inventory of your unused kitchen items:

Blender	$10
Waffle iron	$15
Knife set, new, in the box	$22
Assorted utensils	$30
Hanging spice rack	$10
Ice cream maker	$25
Bread machine	$30
Linens and placemats	$18
Mixing bowl set	$10
Standing mixer	$100
Cake pans	$100
Baker's rack	$25
Assorted glassware	$25
Decorative fruit bowl	$20
Dish set	$25
Cutting boards and serving platters	$25
Total	$490

The kitchen is not the only money pit in your household. Think about this:

_____ CDs bought in a month at $14 each = $_____ × 12 months = _____ spent per year

_____ hardcover books bought in a month at $24 each = $_____ × 12 months = _____ spent per year

_____ video games bought in a month at $17 each = $_____ × 12 months = _____ spent per year

_____ Shoes bought in a month at $45 each = $_____ × 12 months = _____ spent per year

_____ Jeans bought in a month at $35 each = $_____ × 12 months = _____ spent per year

Total it up and see what you could have saved *before* interest. Our calculations can be off by up to 15 percent. But whether your number is correct or off by 15 percent, it's still a hefty amount of money. How would you like to put that in your bank account instead?

Go Team!

Your numbers may not be yours alone. You may need to consider your partner's numbers and goals. Compromise is the name of the game, so team up instead of taking sides. You don't need a "Me versus you" mentality or an "I want to keep my coin collection, but you have to sell your cookbooks" arrangement. Set realistic goals that you are both happy with. Let's say that you both want to start an emergency fund now and have a balance of $3,000. Give yourselves a deadline that is achievable and specific. Instead of saying you want to save it by next year, choose a meaningful date, such as by your wedding anniversary. Finally, break down what you need to do monthly, then weekly, and then daily to meet your goal. A great place to start when sharing goals with someone else is for each of you to write down your top five goals, then compare them *without judgment* and see which ones overlap. Those should be the ones you work on first.

Don't worry if your partner's saving and spending styles conflict with yours. Instead of trying to turn a spender into a saver or vice versa, an impossible feat, try to agree on a set amount that each of you will put toward his or her own goals without the other's input. That way, the spender can spend and the saver can save without conflict.

You Can Do It!

In the coming chapters, you're going to get more organized using the half-and-half method, which will plug your biggest money leaks and de-clutter your home of items to sell. You are where you are because of the actions you have taken. Each item you bring into your home, each time you say yes, whenever you do something and wish you'd done something else, and each time you spend money, time, and energy on something other than creating a rich life for yourself, you shortchange yourself.

The good news is that it is completely within your power to change this pattern, starting today. So let go of any regrets or guilt; forget about the woulda, shoulda, coulda; stop planning, dreaming, and meaning to get to it; and take action. Nothing changes until you do something, so now that you have the time and the energy, it's time to act. Take responsibility. You bought that item, you own it, you kept it, and now you're going to do something useful with it, putting money in your pocket in the process.

I know you can do it, and I'm here to help you. I've seen women whose dining room tables were buried under piles of papers and junk reclaim their dining space. I've watched women whose houses were so cluttered that they were embarrassed to have company take back their space and start to entertain again. I've witnessed women who had little time, energy, or money make the time, work up the energy, and pocket lots of money by clearing away clutter. If they can do it, you can, too.

Sure, it might seem overwhelming, and you might feel a little panicky while in the midst of de-cluttering, but that's normal, even to be expected. I promise those feelings will pass. The trick here is to tip the scales. You can envision something on the other side of the mess that you want more than what you have. The pain of changing is less intense than the pain of staying the same. You really have to want it and be willing to do anything to get it. When you understand this, you are ready. Trying to do it before that point is futile. No matter how big the mess, no matter how high the piles, it is time to take action.

Imagine how your life will be different and who will benefit from your example. How many people will you teach to make their lives better the clean-up-and-get-rich way? You will be happier, less stressed, and more able to enjoy a rich life in ways that extend beyond a larger bank balance. You won't be giving anything up. In fact, you'll get something new. You will feel more connected, and full of self-esteem, confidence, and energy, loving life to the fullest. Now that's a recipe I love!

Caution: Some people from your old, broke, and disorganized world will not understand your new, rich, and organized thinking. Love them anyway, but stick to your new ways. They may or may not get it, but they're not the ones who have to pay your credit card bill or store the new clothes you buy when you go shopping with them. Who knows? You might end up becoming an inspiration to them.

Shop at Home

Think Outside the Box

Most of the time, what we need to get organized can be found in our very own homes. Why spend money on expensive containers, high-end baskets, or drawer dividers when we already have shoeboxes, springtime baskets, and egg cartons on hand that can do the trick?

Take this example from one of my recent shopping excursions. While shopping in the home goods store, I found myself drawn to the box aisle, which had boxes of all shapes and sizes for holding various objects. An aqua blue box caught my eye, and I started to dream of all the ways I could incorporate it into my living room. First, I imagined using the box as the television remote holder, and then I visualized putting it on the bookcase and placing photos inside—just until I scrapbook them, of course. As I came up with a half dozen more ways to use the box, I took it off the shelf. I was thrilled to have stumbled on such a find. There were so many possibilities. It was a perfect size, the perfect color—and it was *forty-five dollars*. Are you kidding me? Surely, the box must be a superspecial box; maybe it came with a wishing genie inside. I read the label, expecting to see something that justified a box costing forty-five dollars, but no, it was in fact just a plain box. Sadly, I instantly lost my love for the box, thinking of all the other things I could do with forty-five dollars. I didn't have to debate it very long; I simply placed the box back on the shelf.

As I reached into my purse for my shopping list, I noticed the shoes in my cart that I'd already picked out to buy. You'll never believe this, but they came in a box that was almost the exact size of the aqua blue box. Perfect! All that I needed was some aqua blue paper. After a quick walk over to the gift-wrap section, for only two dollars I picked up a fantastic aqua blue paper. When I got home, I wrapped the shoebox lid and promptly placed my new box on the bookcase in the living room, where it now sits, holding current photos until one day, hopefully soon, I make the time to put them into an album.

When you stop to think about it, how many times have you bought an empty container, like a box, when you already had a stack of boxes in a pile, waiting to be broken down for recycling? Maybe it's just me, but that seems silly. Why would we spend good money to replace something we already own when we're only going to recycle the one we have? Does that make

MONEY SAVER

Last year Americans spent $7 million on products designed to get them organized. What portion of that came out of your pocket?

good financial sense? Just think of the waste! I am not perfect, and I have been known to splurge on an item when I could have shopped at home, but I try. I continue to remind myself of the goal I have for my bank balance, and this makes it a lot easier to pass up things like that blue box. Now, when I get off track—because it's not a matter of if, but when—I simply let go of any guilt and get back on track. Sometimes I return the item. Why do we spend good money to replace something we already own? Is it because we:

- Want one that looks better?
- Want the newest one?
- Want to avoid going through the trouble of renewing or refurbishing our old item?
- Want to get an item that's like the one our friend just bought?
- Are simply not thinking outside the box?

If you *need* a box, then just about any box will do. But you may *want* a faux suede teal blue box. It's when we prioritize our wants over our needs that we get into trouble. We end up spending money unnecessarily. We need to put sheets on our beds, but we want those with the luxury hotel thread count. We need to make notes on paper, but we want to jot our shopping lists on notepaper that has a magnet on the back. (Keep in mind: Craft magnets costing a dollar for a strip can turn any notepad into a magnetic one.)

Look at Old Items in a New Way

The second part of half-and-half organizing is all about plugging your money leaks by reusing at least half of the items you already own in new and clever ways. I've lost countless hours trying to shove my hand into the utensil drawer in the kitchen when it would not open because the tongs have sprung open, jamming the drawer shut. I'll never get that time back, but I don't have to worry about it anymore. Now I keep the tongs in a cardboard paper towel insert.

It can be difficult, at first, to look past an object's original intended use. After all, who would have thought that an empty laundry detergent bottle could make a perfect nail holder in the workshop, or that a hair clip could be the best way to tame a angle of electrical cords, but they can. We have grown accustomed to a specific item being manufactured to fill a certain need, and we assume that only this item will do the job, but that is not true. Once you look for alternative uses, you'll discover new and unique ways of using just about everything. It simply takes a little practice. Do you think you're not creative? Couldn't you look at an egg carton and see it as a great way to store jewelry? I know you could. It might take a little practice, but you can prove to yourself that you are a lot more creative than you give yourself credit for.

Try this. Look at a rubber band, and tell me three things you can use it for besides its most obvious function. Did you think of three? More than three? I would have said: wrap it around a stubborn jar to get a grip in order to open the jar, wrap it on the edge of clothes hangers to prevent clothing from slipping off, or even wrap it around shampoo or conditioner bottles in the shower to prevent them from slipping out of your hands. See, it wasn't that difficult. You can do this. Look around. You might already be using items in new and creative ways and simply not realize it.

It's time to release your inner crafter. Yes, you do have one. A long time ago, I came to terms with the fact that I would never be Martha Stewart. Although I'm envious of her housekeeping, cooking, and overall craftiness, I know that without my own backstage team, I would never be able to pull off fashioning a bulletin board out of reclaimed wood, no matter how hard I tried. But I can be myself, and being me means that I cheat at crafts. I use double-stick tape instead of a sewing machine to spruce up old items to use again. While it's true that my stenciling may be off center and I seem destined to forget to apply a clear topcoat over my decoupage project, I've made a conscious decision to make it good and *not perfect*. I will never be perfect, and if I expect perfection from myself, I'll only fall short and feel defeated. Instead, I've decided to do the best I can. Being good is enough for me.

I still remember my most favorite project to date. Many years ago, on my way home one day during the townwide bulk pickup week, I drove past a curbside treasure, a unique chest of drawers. It caught my eye because I'd been looking for one just like it. I wondered why anyone would put it out in the heap of junk to be picked up with the bulk trash. I pulled over, a little uncomfortable because I'd never actually picked through a pile of junk before. The chest had all of its drawers, and although they were a little scratched, they seemed fine. I glanced around for just a moment before I loaded it into my trunk. On my way home I started to second-guess myself, thinking, I could have bought a chest of drawers, so what was I doing with someone else's junk? Was it even sanitary to put my stuff in their drawers? Did it make sense to spend time and money fixing this piece of furniture? Did I even know how to make it look like what I envisioned? I pushed aside my concerns and kept my curbside treasure.

As soon as I got home, I researched online to learn how to refinish the piece. I made a list of the few items I needed and posted the list on an online message board. Within an hour, I had replies from board members who invited me to come and pick up the items I needed to complete my project. I dashed out, made my pickups, and got to work. A little sanding, a little painting, some new hardware, and less than four hours later, I had a great chest of drawers. I'd taken this curbside treasure and made it worthy of a high sticker price. Keep in mind, I did not share this story to promote picking up curbside treasures and hiding them away in your basement, only to never get around to those projects. But when you have a need, fill it, from the curb or otherwise.

In case you feel stumped about where to start, here's a list of the most common items I save and reuse to jump-start your creativity. Oh, and before you start saving *every* item I list here, picture two flashing yellow lights with the word *Caution*. This list is not intended to enable you to collect and hoard all of these items for possible future use. I promise you will get more toilet paper rolls and egg cartons, even if you throw some away. These are simply some suggestions to inspire you, so next time you come across an item, you might think, I'll bet I could use this for something.

Baskets. Nothing could be easier than simply cutting the handle off a springtime basket so that it fits on a shelf. These baskets are perfect for all types of storage. Think pantry, bookcase, linen closet, and even your wardrobe closet to get you started.

Berry baskets. Need a desktop or countertop organizer? A place to store hair clips or maybe CDs? Grab a berry basket, and weave a ribbon through some or all of the slots to make the basket décor-appropriate.

Baby food containers. Rinse and dry your baby food containers, then transform them into great organizers. You can wrap a bow around them, add stickers, or paint them so that they match the décor of the room where you'll use them. Get even craftier by attaching a magnetic strip to the bottom and then sticking them on a magnetic board attached to the wall or the inside of a cabinet door.

CD jewel cases. You can attach magnetic strips onto the backs of CD jewel cases to make super photo frames that you can stick on the fridge. Or hot glue a few of them to a long strip of wood and hang it for a classier photo frame. You can even flip the jewel case up and use it as a tabletop photo frame. But that's not all. When you are packing for a trip, store your necklaces in jewel cases so they don't get tangled in transit. You can also use them to scrape ice off your car windshield.

Ice cream containers. Wash ice cream containers well and let them dry. Then paint them, stencil them, sticker them, or cover them with wrapping paper or fabric for limitless storage possibilities. You can also cut them down and use them as drawer organizers or cut a slit in the lid to use it as a coin collector.

Toilet paper and paper towel rolls. Glue the rolls together to make a custom desktop, tabletop, or countertop organizer. A few rolls attached to one another can be used to store pencils, pens, a ruler, lip liners, eyeliners, or even kitchen utensils. Use the rolls to store your children's artwork or your current cross-stitch project. Cut them up into napkin rings that can be used as is or decorated for the occasion. Wind up cords and slip them into the roll, then label the tube so you know what cord is what. The rolls are also perfect for pantyhose storage. Use one roll per pair of pantyhose and label the outside so you can easily identify sandaltoe and navy from black.

Ice cube trays. Use these wonderful drawer organizers in the desk drawer for little things like paper clips, in the dresser drawer for earrings, in the kids' drawers for little toys, or the junk drawer for batteries.

Egg cartons. You can also use egg cartons in your drawers; an open carton gives you a smaller cup section and a larger rectangular section. In a bathroom drawer, use the cups for hair accessories and store larger items like eyeliner pencils in the lid. You can also customize your storage by cutting the carton and only using the cups as you need.

Muffin pans. Turn muffin pans upside down to make a cooling rack. They can also be drawer organizers, condiment servers at a backyard cookout, or coin holders during a yard sale.

Rubber bands. Wind a rubber band at the end of each side of a clothes hanger to turn an ordinary hanger into a pricey non-slip hanger. Cut a rubber band and glue the flat side to the bottom of a bowl, such as a pet's water dish, to make it antiskid.

Shower curtains or plastic tablecloths. Spread a shower curtain or tablecloth underneath a picnic blanket to protect your blanket (and yourself!) from ground moisture. You can also use one to cover the carpet in the trunk of your car to keep it mud and sand free.

Now be honest, are you reading this, thinking, But, Jamie, where in the world will I find the time for craft projects? I'm with you; I know you don't have a bunch of free time to spend wrapping boxes or painting jars. But here's the thing: you can spend either time or money. Oh, and if we calculate it, I'll bet that the time you would spend driving to the store, finding what you need, stopping to make impulse buys, waiting to pay, and driving home would be more than enough time to make the item instead. If you have to go to the store, you are spending time and money. How about spending only time? Think of it as letting your inner kindergartener play. Seriously, when's the last time you got to play with glue and scissors? It can actually be relaxing and lots of fun. Try to involve the family, so that everyone can make an organizer or two. Or maybe you'll want to invite a few friends over to chat while creating something useful. If you are part of a Moneyize Group, you can spend one or two meetings crafting creative organizing solutions.

Don't Let Your De-Clutter Solutions Turn into Clutter Themselves

Once I had a fantastic idea for how to use a great sour cream container with a clear lid. I watched as the container got closer to being empty, and I knew I'd be able to use it any day now. Finally, the day arrived. I scooped out the last of the sour cream but then had no earthly idea what I'd wanted the container for in the first place. From that day on, I've used sticky notes or what I call "life clues," on items that I plan to repurpose. A simple life clue stuck on the item reminds me and everyone else in the house to save it *and* why.

In your quest to de-clutter your lifestyle, follow this one essential rule: if you keep it, you *must* put it to use. Organizing is not a license to keep every sour cream container and paper towel tube you get. You'll get more, I promise. There is simply not enough space to store all of the items you might use someday. Use the item to fill an existing need; don't force a need simply to keep the item. Sure, it might look like a great container that could have a variety of uses, but if you stick it in the closet and plan to use it later, it's called clutter.

Here's what you need to know before you can decide whether the item is a keeper or a recycler.

- What will I use this for today?
- Do I already have one of these?
- If I'm not doing the project today, will I get another item before I do?

Five Ways to Recognize When Your Thriftiness Is Getting Out of Control:

1. You can't fit your everyday dishes into the kitchen cabinet because it is filled with empty margarine tubs.

2. You have to park your car in the driveway because you have boxes in the garage that you plan to use one day.

3. You find yourself digging something out of your neighbor's recycling bin.

4. You seriously consider having a bumper sticker printed up that reads, "I heart egg cartons."

5. You gained a few pounds because you wanted to have a stash of pint-size ice cream containers just in case.

TRACEY'S STORY

During my first organizing session with Tracey, a married mom of two, we decided to reclaim her kitchen. Using a stepstool, I brought down a bunch of dusty stacks of margarine tubs from the top of her fridge. Tracey claimed that they were very useful. I had my doubts. Rarely have I found a "very useful item" tucked away on top of a refrigerator. So I asked a standard organizing question: "Do you remember the last time you used these?" Tracey said she wasn't using them yet, but they might come in handy one day. "Like when?" I wanted to know. She planned to use them for craft projects if she became a Scout mom. Her children were one and three. By the time she became a Scout mom, her home would be overrun with margarine tubs.

"Here's the thing," I explained. "When we continually doubt ourselves by asking 'What if?' we show a fear of not knowing what the future holds. So in this case you may or may not become a Scout mom sometime in the next six to ten years. And even if you become a Scout mom, you may or may not want to make maracas. And even if you become a Scout mom and you want to make maracas, you may or may not even remember that you have these tubs to make them with, and even if you remember, you may not be able to find them when you need them. So, what are you afraid of?"

Without missing a beat, she said, "Not being prepared, and good moms are always prepared." I stopped working and took her hand in mine. I looked directly into her eyes and told her what she had been longing to hear since her son was born: "You are a great mom." Simple yet powerful, those five words brought tears to her eyes.

We kept two tubs for her to use as drawer organizers in the junk drawer, and we bagged up the rest to share with the local day camp. "If and when I'm a Scout mom and if and when we make maracas, I'll save more tubs," Tracey said. "For now, I just want to be able to see the top of my refrigerator." When our appointment was over and I was on my way out the door, she threw her arms around me, hugged me close, and whispered, "Thank you for sharing your gift." I knew she wasn't talking about my ability to organize.

Fill Your Need with Online Resources

When you can't fill your need by shopping at home or curbside, you might find your treasures online, just waiting to be discovered. Two of the most popular sites for locating free items are Craigslist.org and Freecycle.org. You don't need to be a computer whiz to find the good stuff. Just hop online and head over to Craigslist. On the home page, choose your state, then choose the area nearest to you from the list of areas provided. Next, under "For Sale," choose "Free" for a listing of free stuff that's available in your area. You can also use the search feature on the left-hand side of the page. Remember to try a variety of search terms. Although you may call a couch a *couch*, someone else may list it as a *sofa*.

Freecycle is set up as a Yahoo group, so you'll join the group nearest to you. It is simple and, of course, free. As a first-time user, you'll need to register. Select "browse groups" from the menu, choose your state, and next choose your town or county from the list. You can then click "Visit this group," and you'll be taken to the group's home page, where you can read a little more about it. If you are interested, choose "Join this group." Once you complete the registration, an e-mail will arrive from the administrator of your local group.

I don't know about you, but my e-mail inbox is already pretty full. The last thing I wanted was for a bunch of e-mails from Freecycle to be coming into my inbox. To keep my e-mail inbox as clutter-free as possible, I set up a second free e-mail account, and I use that solely for these online searches. Be sure to check the option for the daily digest; otherwise, your inbox will be inundated with every single e-mail that's sent to the group. After you join Freecycle, you will have access to the message board, where you can post a WANTED message. Something simple like:

WANTED: bookshelf (Scotch Plains, NJ)

Looking for a 4–6 ft. bookshelf, new or gently used, any color okay. Will pick up. Thanks!

Then you wait. All the members will see your message, and anyone who has what you are looking for will reply. If it is a match, you can make arrangements directly with that person.

I cannot say enough good things about Freecycle. I've witnessed some amazing stories with one person's trash becoming another one's treasure. In fact, just last Christmas I had some toys, still in their boxes and never even opened, and I wondered who to give them to. Because they would have been the right age for my niece, Kiara, I thought about wrapping them up for her. But I could just imagine how my sister would feel, having to find a place to store all of these new toys, which were extra because I already had my gift for Kiara picked out. I next thought about shipping them cross-country to family members on the other coast, but the shipping cost was too much to bear. Then I remembered one of my favorite resources, Freecycle. I hopped online, logged in, and posted: *for pickup or drop off near 07076 one Barbie Doll with horse-drawn carriage.*

Within an hour I had a reply. It was from a woman who shared her story with me:

> I hope the items you listed are still available, my daughter just loves Barbie. I'd love to give them to her for Christmas, we've had a tough couple of months over here, my husband lost his job and I have been told my department is going to be eliminated as of Jan. 1st. These toys would really be a blessing; I'd love to have a few things for her under the tree.

I replied immediately that the items were hers. We arranged a dropoff, and she got the toys in plenty of time to put them under the tree. A few days after Christmas, I received a note and a photo from the woman, who shared a little glimpse into their home on Christmas morning. The photo was of her daughter, in a plaid flannel nightgown, sitting under the tree holding up the newly unwrapped Barbie with the horse-drawn carriage. She was grinning from ear to ear. She loved the toys and started playing with them right away. She was so thankful for the toys, but I was even more thankful to have played a small role in helping to make a little girl's face light up with one of the biggest smiles I'd ever seen.

Although Freecycle can bring you some amazing moments, it can also be a threat in your organizing endeavors. Here's the deal: whenever you have an item to post on Freecycle, from something as small as a pack of stickers to the entire contents of your home, to anything in between, I ask that you, one, set a timer for five minutes; two, log onto Freecycle; three, post your item in a few words, no fancy photos or marketing ads required; and four, log off and step away from the computer. You are not under any circumstances to start reading about all of the things your neighbors are giving away for free. I'm not kidding; it is too tempting to reply to those posts, agreeing to give a home to those soon-to-be abandoned items. This is *not* the time to bring more stuff into your home. You are purging, not collecting. If you forget and start to peruse ads, the buzzer will go off. This will be your reminder to get away from the computer before you are sucked into saying, "I can find a use for that."

If you don't find what you need on Craigslist or Freecycle, you can also use the "ask for it" feature on Facebook at Facebook.com/marketplace.

A word of warning: It probably goes without saying, but I'll feel better if I remind you that you should exercise caution before revealing any personal information on any online service. In all my years of using these sites, I've never had an uncomfortable experience. Still, I do not post basic information like my address, phone number, and so on, for all of the group members to see. And keep this in mind: if you have any hesitation about going to someone's home for a pickup, then bring a friend with you or ask the member whether he or she will meet you at a local place, such as a library or a café.

When all else fails, sometimes you just have to buy a certain item. Before you do, head over to Buy.com to see what similar items are currently selling for. That way you'll know whether you are paying too much. Then do a search using the terms "[item name or store name] + coupon" to see if there are any coupons you can take advantage of.

Collect the Cash

Where the Big Bucks Are

et your things free! Instead of keeping them trapped in closets and drawers, let them live. Let a toaster be a toaster by getting it out of the back of your pantry and selling it to someone who makes more toast than you do. During my many years as an in-home professional organizer, I've helped my clients unearth thousands of dollars' worth of sellable goods. I have stories about lots of great finds, like the $200 Cabbage Patch doll, the rare bronze buffalo statue, and the one-of-a-kind Tiffany bracelet. What kind of treasures will you find in your home?

Today you're going to clean up the most-cash-guzzling, disorganized places in your home, while picking out junk— I mean, valuable personal items—to sell. Then you'll sell them. These ideas are the very heart of half-and-half organizing. Yet whether it's a book, a piece of sporting equipment, or a pair of designer jeans, you need to cut through the confusion by knowing where to start and what to look for. It can be daunting to find the time to research what the item may be worth, then try to figure out the most profitable place to sell it and how to go about doing this. No wonder you put it off.

Some of you have already begun to collect a mishmash of items you've tossed into a box as you came across them, planning to sell them "one day." Well, this is the day. No more waiting, no more putting it off, no more deciding or debating whether to get rid of these things—now is the time to just do it. Whether you already have a stack of items set aside to sell or you are just now locating your first sellable item, today is the perfect time to begin.

Your Five Boxes: Finding Stuff to Sell

Good news! I've devised a clear-cut plan for finding the clutter that you can turn into cash. Set up five main boxes in an out-of-the-way area, such as in a garage or under a dining room table. Then grab a tote bag to carry with you from room to room to fill up with the sellables. Taking the items a little at a time to a main area is a much easier process than dragging five big boxes around with you. Once the tote bag is full, deposit the items from the tote bag into the five main boxes.

Here's how you should label your boxes:

1. Books: Keep the box small. A big box of books is too heavy to carry.
2. Sell: Stuff in good condition.
3. Hot: Items that are in demand, such as new items with tags or designer names.
4. Value: Items you need to appraise to figure out how much they are worth.
5. Share: Items that are not sellable but have life as is or as parts.

Set a timer for eighteen minutes and go on a treasure hunt, to locate an item or two. This will be your first pass through the house, so you don't have to locate every valuable item hiding in all of the clutter. You can always make a second and third pass later on. After all, you are always accumulating more stuff, so you will have to repeat this process again and again. The key right now is to get started. Once your items go into the five boxes, they are *not* coming back inside the house. Mark your calendar for the time you will need to find and sell the items. Otherwise, you'll let the stuff sit in the five boxes getting dusty, while you keep planning to get to it later.

As you moneyize, I've given you room-by-room cheat sheets so that you know what you're looking for and are careful not to overlook anything. Keep this acronym in mind for inspiration on your money hunt:

Collect the clutter.

Appraise the articles.

Sell the stuff.

Have a rich life.

Overcome any separation anxiety you might feel in parting with these objects by thinking of the money you'll make, the space you'll free up, and the time you'll save. Take a photo of the item, if that will help you let it go.

As you pare down and find things to sell, you might need a Maybe box. This is the perfect solution to alleviate some of your uneasiness about parting with something before you are 100 percent certain you are ready to let it go. Think of the Maybe box as a safety net, the one place where you can store items you are not ready to relinquish guilt-free. The trick is that the Maybe box has an expiration date. Here's how it works:

1. Place items in the box, making a list of the items on the side of it.

2. Tape the box shut.

3. Mark an expiration date on the box (a year is a good rule of thumb).

4. Store the box away.

Should you need anything from the Maybe box during the next year, you can easily retrieve it. Here comes the trick: if on the expiration date you can name anything in the box, *without* cheating and peeking at the list, you can have the item back. If not, then let the whole box go: recycle it, donate it, toss it, just get it out of your home. Trust that you've made a good decision and that if you really needed a certain item, you could have had it. Since you didn't, you'll let someone else use it. Remember, your goal is to pare your possessions down by half, so this is a good start. Are you wondering just how big of a Maybe box you are allowed to have? The answer is, as big as you can carry when it's full and ready to stash in storage.

Who Are You without All of That Stuff?

In "Jamie world," I like to see myself as a weekly party–hostessing, mah-jongg-playing, soufflé-baking, poetry-reading, size-two, scrapbooking queen. In the real world, I may pull off a single potluck dinner a year, have no clue how to play mah-jongg, have never attempted a soufflé (and probably never will), don't really like reading poetry, haven't been a size 2 since maybe ever, and am more of a slap-the-picture-in-an-album-and-move-on kind of scrapbooker. I'm never going to be that person who lives in my head, and the sooner I own up to that, the sooner I can lose the French cooking magazines and the mah-jongg chips or cards or whatever they use to play that game, which obviously I wouldn't know since I've never played.

You need to get a clear picture of who you *really* are today. Then you need to figure out what you want. With those two answers, you can do anything. Sure, discovering the truth may make you feel a little uncomfortable, but the rewards, both personal and to your pocketbook, are huge. Answering these questions honestly might mean admitting right now that you are not the size you wish you were, that you are not going to make the time to read *Pride and Prejudice*, or that you don't know how to knit an afghan. Leaving size 2 jeans on the top shelf of your closet, putting a copy of *Pride and Prejudice* in your to-read pile, or buying skeins of yarn and knitting needles will *not* make your "ideal self" a reality. In fact, living this way will only drain your bank account and make you feel unsuccessful.

Your home needs to be a reflection of you, not of your mother, your sister-in-law, or the newest design magazine. You need to surround yourself with things that make *you* happy. Until you are honest with yourself about whether you are ever going to make the time to read *Pride and Prejudice*, unbox the service-for-twenty china set you were given for your wedding (fourteen years ago), or learn to knit, you will never be truly happy. So if you don't know how to knit, please stop buying yarn during the midnight madness sale at the local craft store. Slowly back away from the baskets of yarn and leave them for someone who knows how to knit. If and when you ever learn to knit, that is when you'll buy the yarn. There's no sense in having it in storage for you to get to later. And if you are not planning to cook five-star French cuisine anytime soon, ditch the cookbooks and toss the soufflé recipes.

These items cost you money and take up space in your home. You are too budget-conscious and busy these days to waste time and money on anything that is not an absolute yes. Maybe you won't ever be a size 2 again, so the jeans can go. Your child is entering college, so the stuffed teddy is no longer needed. You bought that dress and never wore it, so why not sell it to a woman who will use it? Once you make peace with these facts, then you can let go of the items that no longer serve you.

Releasing the guilt about this may be difficult, but it can be done. The great thing is that once you do it, you will be living a fully authentic and rich life in the present. You will no longer be tied down to the past or dreaming of the future; you are living in the here and now and enjoying it!

Although I tend to consider myself a minimalist, I'm far from perfect. I also struggle with what to keep and who I'll be if I let certain possessions go. It took me a long time to finally be okay with letting go of some of the clothing I remember my mother wearing. I picked the few pieces I would wear and boxed up the rest. I felt as if letting these clothes go would be like losing the last piece of my mother. Never again would I see her in the blue vest she wore every day over her nursing uniform. She wouldn't wear the gaudy holiday-themed turtleneck we teased her about on Valentine's Day or her favorite comfy sweater, whose softness I remember when she hugged me close. Then I realized that those memories didn't have to fade and they weren't in the clothing anyway. In fact, I know she'd want people to wear those clothes, instead of having them boxed up, hidden away, and getting messed up in storage.

As I took photos of the clothing, I imagined the person who might wear her blue vest, wondered whether someone might wear the gaudy holiday turtleneck and have a good laugh, or who might get a hug from someone wearing the comfy sweater. Then I let the items live on by selling them to people who would use and love them. The knife set that was too warped and rusty to repair got recycled when I realized that if my mother were here, she would have replaced it long ago. But I kept the porcelain figures of woodland critters that still make me smile every time I pass the bookshelf where they sit. So, who are you and what do you need to let go of?

It can be difficult to answer that question, especially if you have not been thinking about it lately. We can get so busy, dealing with life and tending to others' needs, that our own needs can get lost. So, get out your half-and-half journal and answer a few questions that I designed to help you determine where you are in your life and where you'd like to go. Here's a great way to reconnect with the person you are today. Be honest; your answers to these questions will yield big rewards. Remember, you have no one to impress and no one to answer to but yourself. The answers to these questions are true today. You're not talking about your past or your future. You need to get a clear picture of your current life. Accept who you are today, your authentic self, with no stories, excuses, blame, shame, or embarrassment. Are you ready? Promise me that you'll dream your overall vision without limiting beliefs or boundaries. Think of *yourself*, not of others.

If you struggle to de-clutter, this may be your opportunity to learn something about yourself and to identify what you *really* want. Answer these questions in your journal:

- What three words would you use to describe your home as it is today?

- What three words do you wish you could use to describe your home?

- How will you feel when your home is the way you dream of it?

- List five things you enjoy doing in your spare time.

- List three things you would like to do or would do more often if you had more time or money?

- What size of clothing currently fits you *comfortably*?

- What is one example of clutter that is costing you money?
- What is one example of clutter that is stopping you from accomplishing something?
- What is one example of clutter that is draining your energy?
- What is something you let go of and felt great about sharing or making money from?
- What is the best excuse you use to avoid organizing?
- What is a lie you tell yourself when you are really just putting off a task?
- Give an example of when you doubted something and it worked out.
- List ten things you could sell today without guilt or remorse.
- Does the impulse to hoard or keep stuff come from within or from a fear of going without?
- How would you feel if you started to refer to yourself as organized instead of *busy*, *disorganized*, or whatever other word you use?
- What aspect of the situation did you create, and what can you do that is within your control to change the situation?
- Finish this sentence: "I have clutter because . . ."
- Think about your future: How will it be if you do nothing? And how will it be if you make some changes?

If you are still not sure whether a certain item is a keeper, then ask yourself, "If I had an hour to pack what I love the most, would that item be included in the box?" Remember: clutter sucks the energy, money, and life right out of you and your home.

Don't Trip over These Stumbling Blocks When You Hunt for Sellables in Your Home

Are you still struggling to let go of certain possessions? The process of getting rid of items you've had for a long time can bring up many feelings, almost like being in therapy. You may encounter your past habits of collecting and overthriftiness, your desire to cling to significant people and experiences with mementos of other eras, your all-too-human attempts to create security in an insecure world by squirreling away provisions, and many more motives that are unique only to you. The process of letting go can be a little traumatic, emotionally, but in the end it is incredibly liberating.

Here are some of the most common obstacles that my organizing clients have met with on their money hunts.

When Is the Right Time to Sell?

The right time to sell is when the scale tips and you'd rather be rich than have a certain item reclaim your time, energy, money, space, and interpersonal connections. Even if the object would sell for an extra $5 in two years' time, there is never a wrong time to sell if you are ready to be rich. You may not become a millionaire from selling your garage full of kids' toys or old electronics, but you can improve your bottom line. So, let's put your clutter to work for you.

What If I Love Everything?

How many times have I heard this argument: "But, Jamie, I love it all!" No, really you don't, you just think you do. Everything can't be a keeper, even if it feels like it. *You have to let go to allow money to flow.* If an object never sees the light of day, how much can you really care for it? If you forgot that it was shoved into the back of the closet, how much can you really treasure it? And how much can it really mean to you if you allow it to be damaged in storage? It's selfish to hoard items when they could be used and loved by someone else. A great way to help separate what you really love from what you think you love is to take it all out. Once everything is out of its hiding spot, you can see exactly how much you have. With all of that space freed up, it becomes more difficult for you to put it back because you see how much space you now have.

What If It's Not Only Me?

When we share our lives with people we love, we get them *and* their clutter. You might have most of your possessions in order but may be sharing space with someone who does not. Although you can't force others to clean up, you can encourage them. One of the best ways to do this is to talk about the potential income that could be made from selling those twenty T-shirts. Bringing in extra cash may be all the motivation another person needs.

TRACEY'S STORY *(continued)*

Tracey was frustrated. Her in-laws bought every toy on the market for her children. She and her husband had very different clutter styles, and although she worked all day to organize the playroom, he'd play games with the kids and leave toys all over the place.

Normally, I don't take on organizing jobs where the clients are unwilling participants. As you can imagine, it does not work very well. You can clean up and get rich only when you are ready. If you try before that, you're just spinning your wheels. But Tracey promised me that if her family was not receptive, we'd use our appointments to work mostly on her stuff. Yet once her son found out that we were hosting a yard sale and he could sell unused toys for cash, he was in. We made one bag for charity and many more bags to sell. Tracey was thrilled. When I arrived on our sale day, the front yard was a shopper's paradise. Seven hundred dollars later, Tracey and her family had their space and time back, money in the bank, and new household rules that worked for everyone, such as "clean as you go," which eliminated the all-day-Saturday cleaning marathons.

What Do I Do with the Items That My Family Members Have Left Behind?

You know those boxes of possessions that members of your family left with you? Now's the time to get rid of them. There is no sign on the front of your house that reads Store and Go, right? That stuff is using up your storage space. Plus, it just might be worth something. This project does not have to be tedious. There's no need to threaten people (well, maybe just a little). Instead, you can make it fun: share stories and make it a family event, rather than a dreaded chore. Your family members can help, pick what they want, take photos of other things, and sell the rest. Then you can share the money with them. Think about it: if these items were that important, your family members would have come back for them by now.

What's Hot and What's Not

Rule of thumb: Labels sell! Designer labels, anything from Abercrombie to Zac Posen, are hot, hot, hot. If it's new in the box, with the tags still on, or it comes as a set, it is likely to sell. So is wacky décor. Another hot seller is anything trendy or in the media. When the new *Star Trek* movie hit theaters, *all Star Trek* items, old and new, were in demand. If animal prints are on the cover of *Vogue*, you can bet that animal print accessories are selling like hotcakes. You can check out "What's Hot" at eBayPulse, pulse.ebay.com, to see what is selling right now.

On the other hand, anything that is dirty, broken, smelly, or damaged is *not* hot. You can find something else to do with those items, but they won't be your top sellers.

Dealing with Your Fix It Basket

As I'm typing this chapter on my laptop while sitting on the living room couch, I can see the Fix It basket. This is an idea I've suggested to clients over the years. I wonder whether they are doing any better at actually fixing the items than I am. Probably not. Yet I'm determined to finally see the bottom of the basket, which has not happened in more than a year, so I'm going to look at each item now. I've got:

- A sweater with a missing button. I wondered where this made off to. Fingers crossed that I have the button somewhere.

- A flashlight that needs a bulb. I wondered where the dog-walking light had gone. I decide to fix it.

- A book that needs its cover taped on. I tape it and decide to sell it, disclosing the damage, of course. I lived without it for this long—good-bye!

- A book light that needs a battery. Come on, really? It would have been just as easy to pop in new batteries as to leave it in the basket. Scratch that, you need the itty-bitty screwdriver to get the cover off—ugh!

- A porcelain dog that needs an ear glued back on. I liked him a year ago; now, not so much. I decide to fix it and donate it somewhere, assuming I still have the ear. Yes, there it is, taped to the dog's backside.

- A necklace that's knotted within an inch of its life. Are you kidding me? Baby oil and a toothpick should have this untangled in, oh, an hour or two.

- And, miraculously, the button for the sweater—score!

What a relief to see the bottom of the Fix It basket and to have made decisions about this stuff. So, you have to ask yourself, if you lived without something this long, do you really need it? Decide on a deadline to fix it or get some money for it. Keeping broken items is no longer an option.

When debating about whether to fix something, ask yourself these questions:

- Do I need it?
- Am I lost without it?
- Have I already replaced it?
- How long have I lived without it?
- Do I have another object that serves the same purpose?
- How much time will it take to fix?
- How much money will it cost to fix?
- Do I care about it?
- Will I be sad if I never see it again?
- Can it be used in its current state for something other than its original intended purpose?
- If I saw it, whatever it is, in the store today, would I buy it?

Decide now whether to fix the item or forget it. Do not put it back in the basket. It has to fall into one of these three categories: if it's a "fixer," then fix it today; if it's a "someone else will fix it," delegate or hire it out now; or if it's a "non-fixer," let it go immediately. This does not automatically mean you should put it in the garbage. Even broken things are sellable or swappable or at the very least can save the planet by being recycled responsibly. The truth is, if you care about it enough, you'll fix it. If not, let it go to someone who will either fix it and use it or will use it in another way. Let another person have the joy. You'll be surprised who wants your "junk" and how much people will pay for it.

The Accidental Collector

Are you the victim of an accidental collection? If so, put a stop to it *now* before you can't even walk in your living room.

JENNIFER'S STORY

Jennifer, an accidental-collector client of mine, had one specific goal in mind: to reclaim her living room. It had been overrun by Boyd's Bears. You know the ones, the highly collectable but not terribly valuable stuffed bears. It all started years ago, when a single bear in a bunny suit caught her eye and she bought it with plans to display it in the springtime. Everyone in her family saw the bear and remarked on how cute it was. (Remember the acronym I mentioned in an earlier chapter? CUTE = Can't use this, ever.) So there the little guy sat on the end table in the living room. Soon Jennifer's birthday rolled around, and specially wrapped in flowered paper was another Boyd's Bear. She thanked everyone and sat the new one holding flowers next to the one in the bunny suit. They made a cute pair, and she thought that was the end of it. But no, that was only the beginning of her collection quandary. From then on, for every birthday, holiday, and special occasion, she was presented with yet another Boyd's Bear. Soon her collection ballooned to an overwhelming 102 bears. Well, to be fair, some were bunnies and kittens. She swore that the stuffed animals multiplied in the dark.

That's how Jennifer became an accidental collector. Her living room became part zoo, there was no room to walk, and she had no idea how to let any of them go because they had been lovingly chosen especially for her. We worked together on breaking up the collection; we kept her favorites and separated them into two containers so that she could rotate the collections once during the year. She took photos of the rest and let some go to charity, gave others to a local consignment shop, and put a few of the rarer ones up for sale. This was, of course, after thanking her family and friends for helping to complete her collection.

The On-Purpose Collector

Maybe, unlike Jennifer's accidental collection, your collection was actually amassed on purpose. You enjoy your Lenox bells, your thimbles from each of the fifty states, or your wildlife plates. The thing is, unless you have the space to display your collection and have the time and energy to clean around it, then it is not very much fun. Collections cost money to accumulate, take time to acquire and care for them, and use up lots of space. Now I'm not saying don't collect; just be careful what you collect and be sure you love it. And if your collection is still in the box, then you must seriously reconsider whether to keep it.

I remember helping my godparents move out of their home of thirty years, a huge undertaking that was made even more overwhelming by the 127 containers covered in dust and packed full of items from the Hawthorne Holiday Village. Believe it or not, they didn't even own all of the homes and the figures in the collection—at least, not yet. Because they were moving out of state, they'd hired a moving truck that charged them by the pound. This collection cost more than $200 to move one thousand miles, and it now sits on specially built shelving to support the weight of the 127 boxes. Sadly, the pieces have never been unboxed. You'd need to dedicate an entire room to be able to display the collection. To bring it out just for the holiday season would require that you start to unpack it in July!

As a child, I had two collections, and they were not your run-of-the-mill stamp or coin collections. Oh, no, I had a key chain collection and, get this, a business card collection.

The key chain collection was fantastic. I had sparkly key chains with my name on them, a mini working Rubik's cube, a tiny flashlight, and a fuzzy monkey. At one point my key chain collection had grown to more than two hundred, and each one was better than the next. I never actually put keys on any of them, but I enjoyed showing them off and adding to my collection.

The business card collection, however, is another story. It started while I was picking up takeout food from the local Chinese restaurant, which had a sleek, glossy black business card with a gold panda bear embossed on it. Because I like cute furry critters, I picked one up, and it was all downhill from there. Whenever we went out, I'd pick up a business card. Then my father wanted in on the fun and started to bring me business cards that he picked up during his travels. I had these mini file drawers that were meant for filing business cards, and I'd spend hours filing and refiling the cards, by name, by category, and by company. I had a lot of really interesting ones: some were written in other languages, others had lovely photos on them, and yet others had clever tag lines. Instead of dancing around my bedroom singing into my hairbrush to the latest number one hit or posing Barbie dolls in little jean dresses, I filed business cards. I guess it was a sign of things to come.

They say that if you look back at what you enjoyed doing as a third grader, it holds clues to finding your passion as an adult. I have to say that in my case at least that is 100 hundred percent true. Looking back at being an avid filer so young in life, I think I was destined to become a professional organizer. Over the years I whittled down my key chain collection, giving most of them away as gifts. Today I have my three most favorite ones sitting in my jewelry box. The business cards met the recycling bin many, many years ago. Although I have fond memories of them, I can honestly say that I'm glad they are not taking up space in my life any longer. You may have already guessed I'm not a big collector now. Personally, I find collections to be space hogs. They zap my energy and take a lot of time to clean around and care for. I still remember all of the hours I spent refiling the business cards.

So, if you are the proud owner of a collection, accidental or otherwise, be sure you really, truly love it before you cram it back into the closet. Otherwise, you should seriously consider letting it go. Selling collections can be a huge source of income, and, remember, it is more than okay to break up a set. If you love only a few pieces, keep those and let the rest go.

Beat the Home Office Blues

Improving on the Scoop-and-Dump Method

begin one of my most popular presentations by holding up a messy pile of "very important papers" to the audience and asking whether the mountain of mail looks familiar. Most people laugh. I then add a few more inches of papers to the pile and ask whether that more closely resembles their paper pile, the one that sits on their kitchen countertops, office desks, passenger-side car seats, or even the floor—basically, any horizontal surface that will stand still long enough. Then everyone laughs!

I ask the audience for suggestions on where to stash the scooped-up paper pile. The number one answer is a closet, followed closely by the basement and the guest bathroom's shower. One audience member, Caroline, confessed that she'd had company one weekend and did the scoop and dump. She stashed her stuff in a very safe place—so safe, in fact, that she forgot where she'd placed it until the following weekend when she was preheating the oven for dinner. You can imagine how that story ends. Needless to say, ladies and gentlemen, *do not* try this at home.

So, where's your secret paper stash? The closet? A box in the basement or under your bed? How about in the oven, like Caroline? No matter where it is, I guarantee you that it's costing you money.

By far, paper is clutter problem number one. In addition to the paper that is delivered to you, such as junk mail, bills, statements, catalogs, newspapers, and magazines, there is the paper that comes home with your children: homework, reports, and permission slips. Then there are receipts, clippings, such as recipes, and don't get me started on stuff we print off the computer. We can all agree that paper is a *huge* problem, whether it's on your kitchen countertop, in your home office, or both. Or you may have a migrating paper pile in your home, one that starts on the kitchen counter and roams to the dining room table, then off to a side table, and back. And did you ever experience the ditto phenomenon? That's when one item is placed on a flat surface, and it inexplicably multiplies almost before your eyes.

The very first thing you can do is stop most of your junk mail from coming. Log on to CatalogChoice.org to choose which catalogs you'd like to stop receiving; hopefully, it is all or almost all of them. The fewer you get, the less tempted you are to order more clutter from those books, which are full of all the things you never knew you needed until you saw them in print. Then go to DMAChoice.org and also to OptoutPrescreen.com to stop those preapproved credit card offers and up to 70 percent of other types of junk mail.

Now let's tackle your paper pile. Going through piles of clutter, especially paper, can be more of a treasure hunt or an archaeological dig than an exercise in organization. Hidden in paper piles all across America is lost money. I'm not kidding; there are thousands of dollars to be found. When I say lost money, I mean things like:

- A birthday check left inside a birthday card and never cashed
- A misplaced paycheck that was never deposited
- A gift card that was never redeemed
- Store credits that were never used
- Stock certificates or savings bonds that were never redeemed
- Rebates that were never submitted
- Rebate checks that were never cashed
- Tax return checks that were never deposited
- Loose change

MARYANN'S STORY (continued)

Maryann and Ted found a gold mine in Ted's office. As a gift for Father's Day, she'd booked an organizing session with me. Maryann readily admitted that the gift came with an ulterior motive; she needed to use the office as well and could not find a spot to sit down. When we started, the twelve-by-twelve-foot office was literally awash in papers, the desk was buried under stacks of papers, and the floor was covered. You couldn't take two steps without stepping on some paper. As you can imagine, the job was time-consuming, but with three pairs of hands and a shredder going at full speed, we got through it. Each paper needed to be looked at. It was interesting because the layers of papers on the floor were like an oddball filing system: there were six layers, one for each year since Ted and Maryann had moved into the house. He admitted moving in with high hopes of finally having a dedicated office, but without a clear system he was quickly over-whelmed and simply left the papers wherever they fell. If you lifted two sheets of paper from the floor, you'd find papers dated three years ago; it was sort of like an archae-ological dig.

Ted was a great sport. By the end of only a few hours, we had two bags of shredded papers, and we could see the top of the desk and walk on parts of the floor without step-ping on a paper. Another hour or two into the process, and Ted came across a six-month-old paycheck that he'd never deposited. A minute after that, I located an uncashed rebate check for $150 for a printer he'd purchased. We labeled a box with a big green money symbol, and for the rest of the day whenever we came across loose change, cash, or checks, we tossed them in. By the end of a very long day, Ted had his office space back. He had a filing sys-tem that worked with his "dropper" personality: instead of filing cabinets, we went with clearly labeled baskets on the credenza behind him. All he had to do was drop the paper into the correct basket. We wrapped up the day over a much-needed dinner of cheese pizza as we counted the loot. The box of money yielded nearly $3,500 dollars!

When I've shared this story, some people have com-mented that it sounds like an unbelievable amount of money, but the numbers add up faster than you might think. Here's what we found:

Misplaced paychecks that were never deposited = $1,425

Gift cards that were never redeemed = $400

Mutual fund distribution check that was not cashed = $300

Store credits that were never used = $850

Rebate checks that were never cashed = $320

Random cash = $150

Loose change = $25

Total = $3,470

Ted and Maryann invested a little time in calling the places that had issued the checks, and most of them were reissued, even though some were very old. The couple got their space back, as well as a nice payday.

It can be overwhelming and downright scary to dive into piles of paper. You don't know what you'll find, and chances are you will come across things you forgot to do that are now overdue and that you missed out on. But it's better that you find out now before even more paper builds up. So, how much misplaced money can you rescue? You can start to capture misplaced money today by placing an automatic coin sorter near the entryway of your home, then make it a habit to toss loose coins into it on a daily basis.

In the future, to avoid misplacing money, you need to treat it with the respect that it deserves. In Ted and Maryann's case, it was not that they simply had so much money that tossing away $3,500 didn't matter. Instead, they were so busy trying to make it through each day that they didn't notice the missing money. Although their budget was stretched to the limit, they never thought of that handful of loose change or the stack of paperwork as being all that important to organize. They feel differently now. See how much money you can find in your paper pile and whether you have checks to be reissued. Make the call and try; if the check is for more than a dollar, it'll be worth the phone call to find out.

Home Office Overhaul: The No-Filing-Cabinet System

Whether you have an entire room to use as your office, a multi-purpose room that functions part-time as an office, or merely the corner of the dining room table for office work, a home office can be a frightening place. Maybe you can't see your desk underneath the piles of paper, your computer screen is decorated in layers of sticky notes, and the desk drawers are crammed too full to open.

Here's a thought: take back all of that clutter-covered space that you currently call an office by ditching the filing cabinets, setting up the computer, and adding very little else. When you go with a NFC (no-filing-cabinet) system, you can lose a lot of the junk and streamline the space.

After all, unless you have a full-fledged home business, how often do you really do office tasks at home? You pay bills, fill out a few forms, and have papers you need to store. That's about it. You could have a single rolling cart stocked with all that you need; you could wheel it up to a table or the desk, get to work, and roll the cart back into a closet until you need it again.

Step One: Converting to a Desktop File Box

By now you're saying, "But, Jamie, out of sight means out of mind." I hear you, but papers pinned to bulletin boards or stuck to the front of the fridge don't work either, so where's paper to live? All of those very important papers belong in a desktop file box. Save money by having your essential papers at your fingertips so that you can find what you need to pay bills, make returns, and reconcile credit card statements.

This desktop file box is about eight inches front to back and holds about twenty-five hanging files. Hanging files are much easier to use than manila folders when you are busy and need to grab something quickly. You can slip papers in and retrieve what you need with one hand. You can find these file boxes in home stores, office supply stores, and even online, but before you run out and buy one, shop at home first. There is a good chance you already own a box like this. You might have a plastic travel file box; if so, you can pop off the lid and use that box. Why pop off the lid? Because lids are dangerous. You want to use this box to file, not to pile. You know where I'm going with this. If you have a lid, then on a busy day when you don't want to file, you'll simply place the mail on the lid, and the pile will start to grow. Chances are, you'll never open the file box again. I want you to set up for success, and success is hard to come by if you use a lid.

Success also depends on where you place the box. You will need to see these papers every day, so the box needs to be in the kitchen, *not* in your home office or bedroom. Because it will sit out in plain sight, buy a box or decorate a box that you already have in a way that blends with your décor. It can be made of bamboo, brushed aluminum, fabric, and so many more materials; you can surely find one that matches your décor. With a home for each and every paper that you'd normally leave out as a visual reminder, you'll have your space back.

To set up your desktop file box system, first open the box of hanging file folders. You'll use the folders but not the plastic tabs, so put those to the side. Because they are still good, I probably can't convince you to recycle them, so simply put them aside. Remember, many of these papers just need a temporary home: bills until you pay them, invitations until you attend the parties, coupons until you use them. There's no sense in wasting lots of time creating labels for the folders.

If this idea makes you cringe, congratulations, you are a perfectionist. Your natural instinct is to get out a label maker, create perfect little labels, stick them to the tabs, and stagger them across the file folders alphabetically. Seriously, by the time you do that, the stack of papers will be so high you'll never recover. I promise, no one will want to photograph your desktop box for a photo spread illustrating your organizing abilities. Get over it, lower your standards, and get the job done. You are welcome to go back and perfect it in your spare time. For now, just do something!

Instead of those clear plastic tabs, you'll use sticky notes. I heart sticky notes. They are useful for so many things. In fact, sometimes I wonder whether my obsession with sticky notes is healthy. It's very possible I've crossed a line.

I probably don't have to tell you this, but to make a tab for the file, you'll take a sticky note and stick the sticky part to the inside back of the file. Leave enough of the nonsticky part showing past the edge of the file to write on as the tab. Yes, it is that simple. In a matter of seconds, you'll have a label for your file folder.

Now group similar papers together. Gather all of your pending paper piles from countertops, tables, desks, and the floor. Set a timer for eighteen minutes, and get to work.

No need to worry about perfect file names or creative labels. Instead, grab your sticky notes and a pen. Pick up the first paper. What is it? A bill to be paid? Pop it in a file and label it "to be paid" or "incoming bills" or something else so that you know what's inside. What's the next paper? Another bill? Great, you already have a file. Something else, like a coupon? Slip it into a file and label it "coupons," then move on. Don't worry if you make two files for the same type of paper. You can consolidate the files later. Your goal now is to file, file, file.

Shred as you file, so keep the shredder plugged in and within arm's reach. Preapproved credit card solicitations—shred. A health-care insurance explanation of benefits statement— keep it and file it under "health care" or "medical." This eighteen-minute block of time is for sorting papers. Here's what this time is *not* for:

- Reminiscing over past papers, photos, notes, and so on
- Berating yourself when you find stuff you forgot to do
- Getting overwhelmed by the sheer volume of work to be done
- Decision making
- Catching up on your phone calls
- Watching a show on TiVo
- Checking your e-mail
- Going to do something in another room and forgetting to come back

Focus! This is not the time to think about whether you want to go to the party you've been invited to. Instead, toss the invitation into the "invitations" file, *after* noting the party on your calendar or you'll never remember to go, and move on. Super important: *before* you place anything in a file that is time-sensitive, mark it on the calendar. You're not going to flip through each file every day, so you'll never remember upcoming dates if you don't write them down.

Let's say you receive an invitation to a bridal shower. Before you slip the invite into the party file, make a note of the party on your calendar. If you want to be superorganized, also write down near the RSVP date and the number to call to RSVP. And if you want to be super, superorganized, while saving money, make a note a week or two before the party to buy the gift. This will let you avoid buying the gift on the way to the party and wrapping it in the car, which causes stress and wastes money. You are stopping at a store and paying a premium price for the gift and are also buying a gift bag (when you know you already have plenty at home).

Once all of your files are set up, papers will move into and out of the box. For example, you'll have one file for incoming bills to be paid. When you bring in the mail, stand over the box and slip all of the bills into the "to be paid" file. Make a note on your calendar to pay and mail the bills in enough time for them to reach their destination and be processed on the other end. Tuck the paid stub back into the "to be paid" file for one month until you get the next bill, so that you can check that you were credited properly. Then put the stub into the accordion or expandable file system for long-term storage. We'll talk about this next.

A few months ago, I compared the bill stub listing how much I'd paid to the incoming statement showing how much my account had been credited. It turns out that I was credited $3.67 instead of $36.70 and was hit with a $30.00 underpayment charge. After a quick call to customer service, all was resolved, but I would have lost that money if I hadn't checked.

There are no perfect label names; just write something that will help you remember what is inside. "Important," "pending," "this week," "my stuff," and "urgent" are not the best choices, because so many papers potentially fall into those categories that your file will be five inches thick and you won't be able to find a thing. Instead, use names like "sports schedules," "party invites," "bills to pay," and "health insurance claims." Remember, however, that this is your box and it is filled with the papers you need to reference; no two people's boxes will have the same files. Also remember that the desktop box will most likely be the *temporary* home for some of the papers you'll keep for the long term. For example, tax papers such as

1099s need a home, and, no, it is not the countertop, so they'll get a file of their very own. Once you file your taxes, however, the 1099s will not stay in the box. If they did, the box would overflow in a matter of days. The big rule is, no catalogs or magazines. You can have a separate box for them. If you put reading material in the box, you won't be able to fit any other papers inside. Your box will be unique and only include the file names you need, but here is a list of some commonly used names. Some of them might work for you.

- Receipts
- Recipes
- Bills to pay
- Weekly event schedules
- Medical
- Party invites
- Coupons

The success of your desktop file box hinges on one important step. You *must* skim your file tabs weekly and purge those that are a little too thick, such as recipes, and recycle the contents of the ones that are no longer active, like the bake sale you were in charge of last week. If you only put papers into your box and never take papers out, you will outgrow your box in less than a week. Make skimming your box a routine. Try doing it every Wednesday while you watch a TV program or first thing every Saturday morning or maybe Tuesday during lunch. It doesn't really matter when you do it as long as you do it.

Now you'll be able to find that gift card, coupon, and receipt to make a return, all of which means more money in your pocket. The simplicity of the system is a far cry from your previous backlog of paper piles shoved into bags and boxes in closets and ovens.

Step Two: Creating Your Money Binder

Continuing with the NFC method, here is a simple way to know what accounts you have *without* making a file for each one, which we've already agreed is too time-consuming to maintain. Creating a money binder takes less than twenty minutes and requires no filing. You'll need a three-ring binder, twelve tabbed dividers, three-hole notebook paper, and a three-hole punch.

1. Label each of the tabs with these titles:
   - Retirement
   - Social Security
   - Investments
   - Bank Accounts
   - Household Accounts
   - Credit Cards/Loans
   - Insurance
   - Wills/Trusts
   - Children's Accounts (one per child)

2. Under each tabbed section, make notes about the names of accounts, account numbers, Web sites, log-in names, passwords, and secret questions.

   Retirement: List the name of each financial institution that has any of your investments (401(k), IRAs, etc.). Keep the quarterly and year-end statements here.

   Social Security: Use one tab folder for each person, with the statement that comes from the government.

   Investments: Use one tab per investment account (anything that is not a retirement account). Examples are mutual funds, CDs, stocks, and brokerage accounts.

   Bank Accounts: Use one tab per checking and/or savings account.

Household Accounts: Include your home title or renter's lease, home improvements, and mortgage.

Credit Cards/Loans: Use one tab per credit card, loan, student loan, and anyone else you owe money.

Insurance: Use one tab per policy: health, life, car, homeowner's, renter's, long-term care, and so on.

Wills/Trusts: Use one tab per will, trust, or living will, along with instructions on where to find important keys to other important documents and the lawyers' contact information.

Children's Accounts: Use one tab folder per any minor who has an account.

If you are more tech savvy, then check out Bankrate.com for online calculators and Mint.com for free online money software. Just don't forget to back up your work in case anything should happen to the originals. And if you share these documents with someone who is not as comfortable with the computer, consider printing that person a hard copy so that he or she can feel secure as well.

As you organize the office, box up any potential moneymakers, such as computers and related items: old computers and outdated office equipment, books, and computer software.

Step Three: Using an Accordion File

Keep it or toss it? Who knows? I do. I know exactly which papers you should hold on to and which you should shred. I also know that you are holding on to *way* too many papers, papers you don't need and will never reference again, or the information is available elsewhere.

I mentioned all of those pending papers, and that is half the battle. The other half consists of archived paperwork, such as past tax returns and canceled checks. There once was a time when I would have walked you through setting up an elaborate filing system with manila file folders inside hanging file folders, with one file per category, such as home phone and cell phone, and one for each credit card. Well, those days are long gone. No one has the time or, quite frankly, the interest in maintaining such a filing system for papers we're most likely never going to need again. What a huge waste of time and money. Hanging folders and filing cabinets are not cheap. Did you know that, on average, 97 percent of what is filed is never looked at again? Think of your own file drawers. When is the last time you pulled something out?

And get this; you need only *one* item to create your new system: a thirteen-pocket accordion or expandable file folder. See, I told you that you'd love this system.

Here's how it works:

1. Label each slot of the accordion file folder, one slot per month of the year, and write the year on the outside of the accordion file folder.

2. Fill the current month with important papers, such as stubs from bills as you pay them, pay stubs, bank statements, receipts, explanation of health-care benefits, and credit card statements.

3. Continue to fill the slots for the entire year. When you pay your taxes, add a copy of your return to the thirteenth slot and file the whole thing away.

On average, it is suggested that we keep seven years' worth of backup paperwork, in the event of an IRS audit, so you'll want seven files at any given time: one for the current year and six for six years back. As you add the eighth file, remove the oldest one and shred the contents. These are three great systems to deal with all of the paper in your life. Just set up one at a time. There's no need to panic at the thought of having to set up all three systems simultaneously. Even if it takes you a

MONEY SAVER

- Use binder clips to clip sets of paperwork, and use labels to label each pile: bills, receipts, and so on.

- Create a customized drawer organizer by clipping box lids together with binder clips in a configuration that fits your drawer.

- When priority mail shipping boxes or cereal boxes are cut on the diagonal, they make great magazine holders to stand on a bookcase.

- Toothbrush caddies work as desk organizers in the office.

- A towel rack can hold magazines.

- A cookie sheet hung on the wall works as a magnetic bulletin board.

month to set them up, you'll be ready to handle next month's onslaught of bills, statements, and all those other papers that are coming your way.

Dealing with Virtual Clutter: How to Organize Your Computer

If you've ever wasted time unsuccessfully searching for a document, only to have to re-create it, you know that computer clutter can cost you time and money. Aside from computer documents themselves, there are media files containing music and photographs that can be expensive or impossible to replace. And do I even have to mention the hundreds of e-mails waiting patiently in your inbox?

Some e-mails contain money-saving items such as coupons, and if you can't find and print them, you can't redeem them. It's helpful to regularly go through your e-mail inbox, delete outdated messages, and store others that you want to keep in separate folders within your e-mail program. With most e-mail software, you can create folders or extra "mailboxes" on your computer's e-mail window to hold various categories of messages, such as "friends' e-mails," "ISP server invoices," "coupons," "consumer products," "politics," "jokes," "pet photos," "business-related," and so on. Then, when you are weeding out your inbox, you can save important e-mails in these folders, which won't clutter your screen and will make them easy to find. A bonus is that you will also have the correct e-mail address for each message included with the e-mail, so there's no need to keep updating your address book with e-mail addresses for companies that you use only once in a blue moon.

Beware of clicking unsecured links online. You can inadvertently download harmful software that will destroy your computer, or you may be tricked into providing personal information that leads to identity theft and ruins your credit rating. Before you provide personal information online, always be sure the letter "s" follows "http" in the Web site address line; "s" confirms the site is secure and your information will be encrypted. To save money and get more out of your computer, disconnect the printer. Most of us are simply in the habit of pushing "print" for everything from a cool new recipe to an article we'll never make the time to read. Disconnecting the printer breaks the habit and makes us think twice before we end up with more paper. To save articles the paperless way, create a folder on your desktop called "To Read" or "Articles." Then copy and paste the online article into a blank document, save it, and drag it to the "To Read" folder. Designate one folder per

MONEY   SAVER

If you need to retrieve deleted files for free, try seriousbit
.com/undeletemyfiles.html.

family member as the place where he or she can store documents without cluttering up the desktop. And don't forget to
back up the files; having to replace everything in the event of a
disaster can be costly. If you have a backlog of files to organize
or e-mails to sort, work in eighteen-minute blocks of time: set a
timer and work on that *one* task until the buzzer goes off.

"I Know I Have My Receipt Somewhere, Just Give Me a Minute": Making a Receipt Receptacle

A month or so ago, I was standing behind a woman at the
customer service desk in a local clothing store. She was attempt-
ing to return a shirt. The store clerk asked her for her receipt,
which the women insisted she had. I patiently waited to be called
while a line started to form behind me, as the woman proceeded
to dump the contents of her purse out onto the counter. "I know
it's here somewhere," she claimed. "Just give me a minute."

Lipstick, gum, a cell phone, scraps of paper, an apple, a
small umbrella, a mini sewing kit, lots of loose change, sunglasses, keys, hand lotion, and makeup were scattered on the
counter, but no store receipt for the shirt. Frustrated, the clerk
told the woman she could return it without a receipt but would
have to accept the current price of the item, which was $8.50.

The woman insisted that she had purchased it for $34 only a few weeks earlier. The clerk informed her that it was now on the 75 percent off clearance rack.

The woman agreed to take the loss of $25.50. You probably know what's coming next. For the clerk to process the credit without a receipt, she needed the woman's driver's license. The woman dumped the contents of her wallet onto the counter in an effort to locate her driver's license, and half a sandwich and a small pot lid fell out. Don't ask!

The line continued to grow as this woman's return was processed. Finally, she completed the transaction. She was now $25 poorer than she had been ten minutes earlier, and her aggravation level was off the charts—all because of a small rectangular piece of paper. If she had only used a system to deal with her receipts, this incident would have had a more pleasant outcome.

Without having a method to keep track of those little papers, you may lose money on a return when you are issued only partial credit, or, worse yet, you may opt not to return the item at all.

The solution: a receipt receptacle. Spend no more than five minutes searching your home for a somewhat decorative container. It could be an empty tissue box or a decorative bowl or any other unused container. It now becomes your newly designated receipt receptacle. Leave it near your entryway because you'll empty the receipts from your pockets and purse into it every time you come home. *Do not* place the receptacle in your bedroom or home office. You're too busy to run a single receipt to its new home in a far-off room, so you'll end up putting it down somewhere else, and it will disappear.

Walk into the house and toss the newest receipt in the receptacle. If you need to find a certain receipt during the month, you'll know where it is. Bonus: they will roughly be in date order. At the end of every month, grab the stack and attach it to your bank and credit card statements when you reconcile your accounts.

What's that? You're not up-to-date with the whole reconciling thing? Not a problem, you'll deal with that later. For now, it would simply be nice if you knew where the receipts were.

Fees, Fees, and More Fees

Fees to the right of me, fees to the left. Sometimes it seems like everywhere you look, there are fees being assessed for every little thing. Then there are the pesky "hidden" fees, such as annual fees for credit cards. I've compiled a list of the most common fees, which are avoidable if you become a little more organized.

Convenience fees: These are fees you pay for the "convenience" of, for example, paying your bill by using a check card with an automated attendant. But a convenience fee is usually less expensive than a late fee, so if you are close to the due date, it makes sense to pay the convenience fee. Still, it's money down the drain.

Late fees: Think about the last time you were hit with a penalty for paying a bill late. How much was that fee? On average, they each run about $25. Sure, it might not sound so bad to pay that fee once, but try paying one late fee each month for six months of the year; that's $150.

Overdraft fee: Again, this is another $25 on average, right? So not having a system for recording those debit receipts in your checkbook and reconciling your bank account will come back to bite you, as another chunk of your money is sucked down the drain. Forget about taking advantage of your bank's overdraft protection, which can have huge hidden costs to consumers. Now might be the time to link two accounts so that you don't bounce a check.

Automated teller fees: If you use an automated teller machine that is not at your bank, a service fee may apply. I've seen fees from $2 to upward of $5 applied, so if you withdraw $20 and are charged a $2 service fee, you've lost 10 percent of your own money. Do you see something wrong with this scenario? Being organized enough to track receipts, planning to take cash out only at your own bank, and making the time to tally your receipts really does make a difference. This lost money is easily recaptured, and once you've mastered these basics, you can move on to phase two, which requires more time than organization.

Next, review your choice of banks for your accounts and credit cards in order to comparison shop. This way, you may find a bank with free checking and you can ensure that your bank account(s) suits your needs and does not require a minimum balance for you to avoid being hit with a fee. It's also ideal to pick a credit card with the lowest or, hopefully, no annual fee. And why not choose a credit card that gives you money back as a reward for using it?

If you are not currently reconciling your accounts on a monthly basis, don't get down on yourself. Sure, it's something we all know we should be doing. But just because we know we should do it does not necessarily mean that we are. A task such as reconciling your bank accounts does not have a specific deadline attached to it, and thus is very easy to put off until you have an overwhelming stack of statements to review. By that time, who even remembers what you bought when? Once you start reconciling your accounts, you'll be surprised to catch accidental (or not so accidental) double billings, monthly recurring charges for things like subscriptions you forgot you're paying for, and so much more.

If you are looking to get on track with your new reconciling project, here are the steps I suggest:

1. Shop at home to locate a nice container that you can use to collect your statements for the month.

2. To the container, add a calculator, a pen, a pencil, scrap paper, and a stapler.

3. Place the container near where you bring in the mail so that you can toss in statements as they arrive.

4. On your calendar, mark off an hour once a month to get the job done.

5. Locate this month's statements and add them to your container.

6. On the date you marked on your calendar, set a timer for sixty minutes and grab your container and your receipt receptacle.

7. Match up the month's worth of receipts to the correct statement; for example, Visa charge receipts to the Visa bill and ATM receipts from the checking account to the checking account statement.

8. Ensure that all of the charges on your accounts are correct and that your bank statements add up.

9. If everything works out, store all of the month's statements with their corresponding receipts in the slot labeled for the correct month in a twelve-slot expandable file folder.

10. If there are any discrepancies, keep them out of the folder and make the appropriate phone calls to resolve the matter. File the papers only when they are correct.

That's it, simple and doable. No convoluted filing systems to deal with, no drawers of manila file folders packed to the gills, and, best of all, no more "to be filed" piles hanging out on top of the filing cabinet. C'mon, don't act like you've never made one. We've all made a pile to file later, but most of the time, later never comes.

Coupons, Rebates, and Points—Oh My!

We've all done it—we've all spent time clipping coupons and then never used them. What a waste, especially if, before the coupon expired, you ended up buying the item at full price while the coupon sat in a kitchen drawer or at the bottom of your purse.

Being disorganized can cost you 35 cents here and 75 cents there, which on double-coupon days could translate to 70 cents and $1.50, but then you'd have to remember to shop on those specific days.

You may argue with me that your time is too valuable, and you're not going to spend time clipping coupons. You may prefer to print your coupons off online sites. Yet the valid coupons may be lost in your already jammed e-mail inbox. Even when you do print them, you need to remember to use them. The good news is that it's not all about the coupons. You may opt to start somewhere else in the organization process, so that you can find money that is currently being lost in other areas.

Simply having your store loyalty tag with you when you check out can add up to big savings. Typically, stores require you to present your tag to take advantage of special sales and discounts. Nowadays, stores do not seem as willing to swipe the manager's card; they want you to carry yours with you.

To ensure that you have the coupons and the store tags with you when you are in the store, which is when you need them, here are a few suggestions. Fill a single key ring with all of your discount tags. This keeps your house key ring more organized, and you can find the store tags whenever you need them.

I keep my store coupons in the car. Carrying them around in my purse is a waste of the space in my small purse when I will only need the coupons on errand day, but leaving them at home ensures that I'll never have them when I need them. So I strapped a CD holder to the sun visor in the car; then instead of filling it with CDs, I slip the coupons into the slots.

Still, there will most likely be a day when you are at the store without the coupon or you simply forget to hand it to the cashier. Or maybe you'll buy something, only to see it for less in the weekend sales flyer. This is not a problem now that you've honed your organizing skills. Simply take the receipts and the coupon or the flyer to the customer service desk within thirty days of your purchase. Most stores will give you the cash back for the difference, no questions asked.

No conversation about coupons and discounts would be complete without mentioning marketing companies' diabolical plan: rebates. Did you know less than 21 percent of people actually correctly complete and mail in the rebate forms? No wonder companies love them; just think of all the free money they get. I'd rather *you* pocket that money; after all, it is owed to you.

But I know that in the rush of life, most of us leave the rebate form out on the kitchen counter, planning to get around to it later. Later never comes, though, and the rebate form gets lost under a pile of other very important papers. If you are lucky enough to find the time to fill it out, you also have to hunt down the UPC code and the original receipt. Good luck with that. If you are able to pull off that minor miracle, you're not finished yet. You still have to get all of this into an envelope, apply the correct postage, and pop it in the mailbox so that it can be postdated by the deadline.

You'd think the saga would end there, but not so fast. You have to remember that you are expecting to receive the rebate and then follow up if it does not arrive within the allotted time. Manufacturers are betting on the fact that you'll procrastinate about mailing in your rebate; they hope you'll forget about it altogether until it is too late. But with your newfound organizing skills, they won't be able to take advantage of you any longer, and you'll get the money you deserve. Rebatetracker.com is the perfect place to track the status of all of your rebates.

Finally, let's chat about those loyalty punch cards. You know the ones I mean: buy twelve sandwiches and get one free, purchase ten drinks and the eleventh one is on us. Sure, it sounds like a good plan, but where are you supposed to keep that loyalty card until you reach the magic number? If you misplace the card, you are misplacing $3 to $30, depending on what the card is good for. So, these cards are important and need to be treated like cash, because that's what they are. Dedicate a single section of your wallet to these cards. If you ever forget to get a card validated, try bringing your receipt back to the cashier the next time to ask for the missed punch.

You'll be amazed at how these simple changes will result in cash back if you start today. Check out the manufacturers' Web sites of the products you use to see what offers they have. Here are a few more cost-cutting ideas:

Go to the Web site *before* heading out to the store, the local pharmacy, the craft store, and so on, and check for sales flyers and printable coupons or search "store + coupon."

Shop Thursday night because that's when stores typically set up the weekend sales. Tuesday through Thursday are the best days to get online deals.

When shopping, bring the ad for the store to match the item's price; most stores will.

Whenever possible, shop in groups. For example, if you need a new fence, ask your neighbors if they need one too. When several people are buying the same item, many times a company will give you a group discount.

And check out my list of favorite Web sites to see which ones will be your new favorites for coupons and cash back.

Printable Coupons and Coupon Codes

Coolsavings.com

CouponCabin.com

CurrentCodes.com

Dealcatcher.com

Dealio.com

Offers.com

RetailMeNot.com

WowCoupons.com

Cash-back Web Sites

Bing.com/shopping

Ebates.com

Fatwallet.com

Shopping Bots

Bizrate.com

Pricegrabber.com

Pronto.com

Shopping.com

Shopzilla.com

Trackle.com

Conquer Your Kitchen Clutter

The Heart of Your Home Is Draining Your Wallet

I t all started with my knife drawer. I counted the knives, and I had thirty. No one needs thirty knives unless she is planning to open a cooking school. Because I wasn't, some of them had to go. I kept one of each size and was left with five, not to mention the large drawer I reclaimed in my kitchen. Whew! What a relief.

After I finished with the knife drawer, I was jazzed to see what other space I could free up. Hmmm, I've only used that humongous popcorn maker once or twice a year. Who was I kidding? That popcorn maker made enough to feed an entire theater full of moviegoers. And don't even get me started on the panini press, the waffle iron, the chocolate fountain, the slushy maker, and the s'more roaster. As much as I like to tell myself that I'm a panini-pressing, waffle-making, s'more-roasting kind of person, I've never pressed any panini. I buy my waffles in the frozen foods aisle and make my s'mores in the toaster oven. It's just easier that way. Have you ever tried to get melted marshmallow out of the carpet once it's dripped off the skewers they give you? All of those small appliances, going, going, gone. I sold, donated, or simply gave them away. Once I was honest about who I am, I got my space back, while making other people really happy and putting money in my pocket.

The kitchen is the heart of your home, a sort of command center: the area where you prep, cook, sort mail, entertain, help your children with their homework, sometimes pay bills, and so much more. The kitchen is the most commonly used room, and clutter makes it a really big clutter-cash trap. There's the mail-and-paper pile on the countertop; the freezer and the fridge full of uneaten food; the pantry with six jars of pasta sauce, yet not a noodle in sight to pour it on, so instead you order takeout; not to mention the grocery shopping and the unused coupons. And don't get me started on all of those recipes that we clip but never prepare and the sellables sitting on the counters and hidden in the cabinets. The solution: you need simple systems to keep your kitchen running smoothly.

You're going to whip the kitchen into shape by organizing key areas. I'll give you the scoop on what you can sell, so get those sellables boxes ready and let's cook up some savings.

Start with Your Cabinets and Drawers

First, you're going to clear the cabinets and the drawers and find stuff to sell. You'll also make space to store items you do use so that you can find them again. Group similar items together, and pare down the total contents of your cabinets and drawers by half. If the utensil drawer won't open or close without your pushing down the items inside, keep your favorites in the drawer and store the others in an excess box, so that when you need a new utensil, you can retrieve it from the box and toss the old one in the sellables box to make some cash.

Now, starting with the first cabinet, you'll go across the room from top to bottom. Without a system, you would jump from spot to spot and ultimately accomplish nothing. Organize high and low, in the backs of cabinets and drawers, and box up your sellables as you come across them. What counts as a moneymaker? How about bakeware and baking supplies such as rolling pins, cookbooks, excess glassware, flatware and linens, knives, pots, pans, specialty utensils like avocado slicers, dishes, grilling tools, kitchen utensils (think rubber spatulas), and serving bowls, platters, and pitchers.

Here are some ways to rethink your drawer and cabinet organization:

- Use binder clips or clothespins to seal a bag of leftover chips.
- Create a customized drawer organizer by clipping box lids together with binder clips in a configuration that fits your drawer.
- Berry baskets can hold those little utensils that slide around in the dishwasher. Rubber band one to the top rack.
- Use a pantry packet organizer to hold packages of seasoning mixes or drink mixes in your cupboard or to organize your junk drawer.
- Baby food containers can hold spices.
- Stack your plates on a file sorter.
- Hang pots and pans on the wall with S hooks.
- Install a spring-loaded curtain rod vertically between two shelves to create a slot for easy-access bakeware storage.
- Use tissue boxes to store a dozen plastic shopping bags or place the boxes upside down to create tiered shelving in the pantry.

- Paper towel rolls will hold cooking tongs closed in a utensil drawer.

- Baskets are great multitaskers. They can be used to hold kitchen utensils, items you need to set the dinner table, and many other things. You can also put your cleaning supplies in a basket, which you can carry from room to room. Create makeshift storage for oversize items by placing a basket on a rolling cart.

- Stacking shelves are ideal when you have the height but not necessarily the width for storage. The shelves come in widths that range from extra small (six inches) to jumbo (more than a foot) and are made of heavy-gauge wire coated in plastic, rubber, or stainless steel. They're great for dishes, canned goods, and spices.

- Undershelf baskets, which hang from existing shelves, allow you to make use of previously wasted space between the tops of your canned goods, for example, and the shelf above. The baskets come in various depths, so you can use them to store everything from placemats to cookbooks.

Make Your Kitchen Counters Clutter-Repellent

We've already determined that horizontal surfaces are magnets for clutter, so it is no real surprise that keeping the kitchen counters and table clutter-free is a constant battle. The good news is that it's a battle you *can* win without resorting to setting the table with the fine china to prevent people from putting stuff down, although that's not an altogether bad idea.

Let's start with the appliances you use at least once a week. Those are the only ones you should consider leaving out, so your stand mixer does *not* get to stay out. If you have any appliance that you haven't used in the last year (or ever)—it's a sellable. Toss it in the box.

You're going to find a bunch of items that will make money for you when you arrange the kitchen in a way that works for your lifestyle. Do you drink coffee in the morning? If so, place filters, coffee grinders, mugs or travel mugs, sugar, and spoons near one another, so that you can go to one spot for your cup of morning joe. Do you have a sno-cone maker, a s'more melter, or a fondue set that you don't use? Toss them in the sellables box— they're your moneymakers. Place your utensils near the stove, potholders near the oven, and so on. Recycle or toss broken or worn-out utensils. Not sure whether you're ready to sell the garlic peeler? Then try this: dump the items from the utensil drawer into a large box, and leave it on the countertop for a week. As you use an item, put it away where it belongs. Anything that's left in the box after a week is either a duplicate or is not necessary. Add these items to the sellables box.

What other moneymakers are you searching for? Small countertop or handheld appliances can bring in big bucks. Specialty kitchen gadgets and cookbooks are always popular; so are collectibles like teapots.

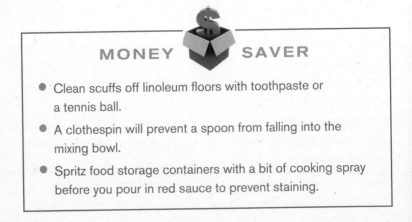

MONEY SAVER

- Clean scuffs off linoleum floors with toothpaste or a tennis ball.
- A clothespin will prevent a spoon from falling into the mixing bowl.
- Spritz food storage containers with a bit of cooking spray before you pour in red sauce to prevent staining.

Look in Your Fridge for Cold, Hard Cash

Organizing your freezer and fridge is just like finding a hundred-dollar bill in the crisper drawer. You'll then find it easy to see the ingredients you have so that you'll know what to serve and what to buy, and less food will end up uneaten in the trash.

We've all experienced a UFO (an unidentified food object) in the fridge, whether it was a takeout container from weeks ago or a fruit or a vegetable in the bottom of the crisper drawer. Do you want to know the oldest thing I've ever found in someone's fridge? A twelve-year-old bottle of Italian salad dressing.

The problem is that when you don't know what food you have in the fridge or don't have a plan for when and how to eat it, the food goes to waste. So, basically, you're throwing money away. Just the other day I bought a bunch of chives. I didn't have a well-thought-out plan for them. I simply saw them in the produce section and thought I might be able to do something with them. I spent $2.39 on those chives, which sat in my fridge for more than a week. Every day I saw them and thought, I have to figure out something to do with those. But I never did. You'd think I would have baked up some potatoes and used them as a topping or at least frozen them, but no, I let them wilt. Then they went from wilted to just plain disgusting. I ended up having to throw my $2.39 into the garbage. As you can imagine, I did not feel very good about it. I kept thinking that I knew better; I knew how to make a plan and shop from a list. But there was something about those chives that tempted me.

If you've ever done the same thing, maybe not with chives, but with some other food that you had to toss because you forgot about it or bought it and never used it, I promise you there is a simple solution to put that money back in your pocket.

You need a fridge makeover. You have to be able to see the food so that you can remember to use it. Here's a quick and easy way to clean and de-clutter your fridge:

1. Grab a garbage can, then turn the temperature-control knob inside the refrigerator to "off."

2. Fill your sink with soapy water.

3. Take everything out of the fridge. As you pull it out, decide whether it is something to keep or to toss. Check expiration dates carefully. You might have some salad dressing that's older than you think.

4. Pull out and place into the soapy sink water all of the removable pieces, shelves, and drawers.

5. While the pieces are soaking, wipe out the fridge, including the sides and the rubber gasket.

6. Replace all of the shelves in the best configuration by testing the spacing, using the tallest item you'll need to store, such as a water pitcher. That way, you'll be certain it will fit.

7. Turn the refrigerator knob to the recommended setting, which is usually a little below the middle point, keeping the fridge at a cool 38 degrees. Line the fruit and vegetable drawers with a towel or some paper towels to keep them clean. Place a sheet of bubble wrap in the drawer as well to prevent bruising.

8. Consider placing a box of baking soda on a back shelf for freshness. Purchase the one with a perforated window or poke holes in the box lid instead of pulling off the lid, to prevent spilling if it tips over.

9. Put back all of the food items. Try grouping similar items together. For example, put all drinks on one shelf, all condiments together, and so on. Before storing away sticky

bottles, place each one in a muffin foil to contain any mess before it drips down onto the shelves.

10. As you go along, make a list of the items you need or want to use. Then you can plan a menu for the week, using the items before they spoil.

11. Wipe down the outside of the fridge, including the top and the handle. Consider placing a layer of clear wrap over the top of the fridge to keep it clean. Then you can replace the clear wrap as needed.

12. To be even more organized, place all of the items that are used for one task in a bin that you can pull out at one time; for example, all of the ingredients needed for making sandwiches.

13. You might also consider placing a lazy Susan on one of the shelves so that you can easily reach small items.

14. Now that you have an organized fridge, keep it that way by wiping up spills as they happen and placing items in the right area the first time, keeping similar items together. And make it a new family rule to add items to the grocery list when bottles or packages are half empty.

Are you overwhelmed by too many leftovers? Here are some ideas to make better use of them, so that they won't go to waste.

- Store leftovers in single-serve portions to make them more convenient to heat up and eat.
- Check StillTasty.com to see how long you can eat leftovers before you risk food poisoning.
- Designate one shelf as the leftover shelf so that everyone knows where to look for a snack or a quick meal.
- Use a dry-erase marker to label leftover containers.
- Store leftovers in the right-size container to keep as much air out as possible; air is what spoils food the quickest.

And whenever appropriate, store containers upside down to create a vacuum, which prevents more air from touching the food.

- Jot down the leftover food you have on your menu board so that you will remember that it is available to eat.

Can I really *freeze that? Yes, you can!*

Bread

Brown rice

Butter

Coffee

Cooked pasta

Egg nog

Flour

Milk (Take one cup out because it will expand.)

Nuts

Veggies

Wheat germ

Insider Freezing Tips

- Label the containers, and place bookends in the freezer to keep food from tipping over.
- Ice cube trays are perfect for freezing individual cookie dough portions. Freeze herbs before they go bad and leftover juice from canned fruit to add to iced tea.

Make Your Pantry Pay Off

Not all of us have the luxury of a walk-in pantry. Yet no matter how much or how little pantry space you have, you can make it pay off. When it's stocked with the basics and set up in a way that you can find what you need when you're looking for it, this results in less wasted food. Plus, meal planning, cooking, and grocery shopping are easier and will cost less.

1. Empty the pantry shelves of all items by moving everything out.

2. Clean the pantry shelves and wipe them dry with a towel.

3. Line the shelves with clear wrap that wipes clean and is easy and relatively inexpensive to replace if necessary.

4. Plan pantry use by categorizing the shelves into prime and nonprime storage areas. If possible, prime storage at eye level should be for the most often used items.

5. Further categorize the storage by grouping similar items together. For example, use one shelf for baking items, another for canned goods, and another for pasta and rice.

6. Mark these categorized shelves with sticky notes denoting their contents.

7. Begin to fill the pantry by placing items on the appropriate shelves.

8. Keep a bag handy to fill with unopened food that you'll never use, to donate to a local food pantry.

9. Make a few lists as you work.

   • A shopping list of items that you're missing or you're low on.

   • A list of containers, trays, or extra shelves to make your pantry more useful.

   • A list of pantry items that you have on hand and need to work into a meal soon.

10. Place small items (such as mixes) into a small box or plastic container, a berry basket, or even a small bag

tacked to the inside of the pantry door to keep them together.

11. Designate a lower shelf for paper storage, and place all napkins, paper towels, and paper plates together.

12. Prevent infestations by insect pests by placing a few bay leaves loose on the shelves near items such as flour, pasta, and cereal.

13. Keep some heavy items, such as soda bottles, on the floor or on a lower shelf.

14. If you have extra wall space in your pantry, consider hanging up hooks, a bulletin board, or other helpful organizing items.

15. If you cannot fit everything in neatly, consider removing some nonessential items for storage elsewhere. For instance, store paper goods in the garage or extra soda elsewhere.

16. If necessary, add battery-operated lighting. You can't use what you can't see.

17. Stash a stepstool nearby to help you easily reach top shelves. You can't use what you can't reach.

18. Step back and admire your newly organized pantry. Then keep it that way by putting items back where they belong when you cook meals or empty bags after a shopping trip.

If you have no pantry space, don't panic. Use a space that will function as a pantry, such as a cabinet, a drawer, a cupboard, an armoire, a baker's rack, or any other convenient space. You can even buy a slim-line pantry on wheels that rolls into only eight or twelve inches between the fridge and a wall.

Insider Pantry Tips

- Rotate items to keep food fresh; always place the newest foods in the back.

- Date your items. Keep a permanent marker handy, and write the date that you bought an item on the package.

- Decant large amounts of liquids into smaller, more manageable containers. There's no need to struggle with a five-gallon jug of oil; pour some into smaller, more user-friendly bottles.

- Store whatever foods you can in airtight containers.

- Try keeping a snack basket handy, where you can store individual portion sizes to grab on the go.

- Keep up to twelve weeks' worth of food on hand *if* you have the room to store it.

- Tack up a menu board where you can list the snacks and the leftovers you have on hand, so that they can get eaten before they go bad. If you pick up a bag of Veggie Booty, you need to remember to eat it before it gets stale or turns into a science experiment.

Take Charge of Your Junk Drawer

Junk drawers can quickly get out of control. They become so jumbled, you can't find what you need, or they get so overstuffed, you can't even open them because something like a tape dispenser is in the way. You need to keep those odds and ends handy, but how convenient is it when you can't even open the drawer? Here's a quick fix to keep your junk drawer junk-free.

1. Start by emptying out the drawer and placing everything where you can see it. Then clean the drawer; get those crumbs, crayon nubs, and scraps of paper out of there.

2. Identify any objects that should live elsewhere, things such as children's toys that belong in their rooms, little-used tools that are better kept in toolboxes, and so forth.

3. Add drawer dividers. Use a variety of box lids to create a custom organizer, and use paper or binder clips to attach the lids to one another so that they won't slide around the drawer as it is opened and closed. You can even use an egg carton as part of your custom divider; the cups make great storage receptacles for tiny items such as twist ties and camera batteries.

4. Put back into the drawer those items that you know you reach for at least weekly. If an item is not used often, it probably does not deserve a space in this drawer. There's no need to keep a whole set of tools in the junk drawer, but a screwdriver and a little hammer make sense. Are you unsure about what you use most often? An easy way to find out is to dump the contents into a box and leave the box on the counter for a week. Whenever you reach for an item to use, return it to the drawer. At the end of the week, you'll have a very clear picture of what's used frequently and what's not.

Use clear containers, even zipper-lock bags, to corral small items such as birthday candles, so that you can see what you have at a glance. Avoid overcrowding by storing the excess elsewhere. No one needs a four-pack of clear tape in the junk drawer. Place a single tape dispenser in the drawer, and keep the remaining three in a box labeled "extra office supplies."

The Frugal Family Table

Do you feel as if you should be serving up a piping-hot meal that contains all of the food groups every night? Now be honest, in the last week how many nights did you serve such a meal? Somehow, it seems as if mealtimes should be easier, but they roll around so quickly. Without a plan, we waste thousands of dollars on drive-through and takeout meals or from stopping at the store to pick up ingredients to make a single meal.

Just last week I was in a high-end bread-and-sandwich shop at dinnertime. The woman in front of me was standing with a boy in a baseball uniform and a girl in a ballet leotard. She told each child to pick out a meal. After ordering her own meal and a takeout meal for her husband, she'd spent $47, most of which was for salad! I happened to overhear her talking with her daughter, saying she hoped it would be good because it seemed a little pricey. At $47, I'd say so. I was ordering myself a dinner, too, and I also chose a salad. Salad is so easy to prepare, but I spent $14 on it—ugh! So, I never claimed to be perfect. I'd fallen off my meal plan for the week, but I got right back on it.

When you don't order takeout, haphazard grocery shopping on a night-by-night basis can also be expensive. While you're in the store picking up ingredients for that night's meal, you'll buy other food, too. And you won't have your coupons or earth-friendly canvas shopping bags with you. All of this can leave you feeling inadequate, while it increases your credit card balances and drains your bank account.

TRACEY'S STORY *(continued)*

While I worked with Tracey and her family, one thing became clear: she longed for a deeper connection with her children, who were growing older too quickly. She wished they could have family dinners around the table, like the ones she'd had while growing up. The trouble was, she could not see her table underneath everything that was piled on it, so the family ended up eating in shifts on tray tables in front of the television, which did not promote conversation.

Our first goal was to clear the table, which was mostly covered with piles of paper; in doing so, we reclaimed lost money. We worked on her kitchen, which meant finding lost money in the pantry and the fridge. We stopped calculating her savings when we hit $300. One thing we knew for sure was that with a clear table and a meal plan, Tracey and her family could have dinners together again and reconnect with one another. That was priceless.

What should you do when it's time to answer the age-old question "What's for dinner?" Plan your meals in advance. Wait, don't turn the page. Hear me out. Meal planning is not nearly as overwhelming as it sounds, I promise. And if you're like me and saying, "But, Jamie, I have no idea what I'll feel like preparing or eating two weeks from tonight," no problem. This plan is flexible, so you don't have to know whether you'll want eggplant Parmesan on October 28. If you are willing to put in just a little time and effort, planning your meals in advance can become much easier and more organized and will leave you with time, energy, *and* money to spare.

When you plan meals in advance, you will:

- Save time while grocery shopping and avoid running to the store for items you forgot and, while you're there, picking up impulse buys.
- Save money by preparing meals at home instead of buying takeout and eating out, which are pricier.
- Eat healthier foods, because home-cooked food is usually better for you than takeout is.
- Never be confronted with the dinnertime dilemma of trying to figure out what to make at five o'clock when you and your family are already famished.

What, exactly, is a meal plan? Quite simply, it's a list of meals you plan to prepare over a specific period of time. I'll tell you how I work out my meal plan. It might take you a little longer the first couple of times you do it, but after a while it goes fairly quickly and saves you lots of money and stress.

Master Meal Planning

You're going to plan meals for two weeks at a time. Any more than that, and planning becomes a challenge. Any fewer than fourteen days, and you'd be going to the store too often. Having themes makes meal planning easier. Grab a sheet of paper, and jot down seven themes or categories of meals that you and your family enjoy. For example, in my home we have Slow-cooker Sunday, Stir-fry Monday, Chicken Tuesday, Mexican Wednesday, Pantry Potluck Thursday, Seafood Friday, and Italian Saturday.

Having a general idea means that if Tuesday is chicken, you'll always know to defrost the bird on Monday night. I plan pantry potluck on Thursday, which is a nice way of saying "leftovers and any dish that will use up ingredients from the pantry." I chose Thursday because that tends to be the busiest day, and a single hot meal is not easy to get on the table. Having a plan with an overall theme also means you are narrowing your choices. You can focus on making one meal within that theme, rather than being overwhelmed with limitless possibilities of what to cook. Instead, you will always know that on Friday, dinner will include some sort of seafood.

Next, mark the days on your family calendar when you know you will be going out to eat. Maybe you have a date or an important meeting, or you will be away on business. Jot down on these days the fact that you *won't* be making a meal. When you are finished, two weeks of your calendar should look something like the calendar below. This is also the time to mark any days that you plan to get takeout, although with a simple meal plan in place I think you'll find yourself doing this less.

Sunday	Monday	Tuesday	Wednesday	Thursday	Friday	Saturday
	PTA meeting: Takeout	4 p.m. karate	8 p.m. book club			1 p.m. bake sale
Going to the zoo with the kids, will be eating there	7 p.m. scouts	4 p.m. karate	Dinner with Joan and Kelly @7:00	7 p.m. women's club mtg.		

Next, pull out the grocery store circular and coupons to check out the supersales, to help you decide on the meals you want to prepare. You may have a file in your desktop file box labeled "grocery shopping" where you keep these items. Remember your master themes, and jot down the meals on the calendar for two weeks. Are roaster chickens on sale? You can roast one on Tuesday, also known as chicken day, and use the leftovers on pantry potluck Thursday for BBQ chicken pita pizzas. Now your calendar will look something like this:

Sunday	Monday	Tuesday	Wednesday	Thursday	Friday	Saturday
Lasagna	PTA meeting: Takeout	4 p.m. karate: Chicken Marsala	8 p.m. book club: Tacos	Vegetable noodle soup with garlic bread	Salmon and rice	1 p.m. bake sale: Eggplant Parmesan
Going to the zoo with the kids, will be eating there	7 p.m. scouts: Stir-fried beans and vegetables	4 p.m. karate: Roasted chicken	Dinner with Joan and Kelly @7:00	7 p.m. women's club mtg: BBQ pita pizza	Grilled shrimp and vegetable skewers	Spaghetti with meatballs

If the store circular does not provide enough inspiration, try these tips. Look through all of those recipes that you've clipped but never tried and that stack of unread cookbooks. Better yet, flip through takeout menus from restaurants. I get my best ideas by looking at the menus to see what I would order and then deciding to make it at home instead. It's cheaper and the dish can be customized to suit people's preferences, such as extra olives or no onions. Copycat-Recipes.net is a great source for chain restaurant recipes.

Always have a backup plan of a frozen meal or a quick and easy meal that you usually have the ingredients on hand for. I have a hot weather and a cold weather emergency meal. My cold weather meal could not be easier; I make a yummy soup by filling a soup pot half full with V8 juice, then topping it off with veggie broth. I next dump in frozen and/or canned veggies, such as green beans, corn, potatoes, and whatever else I have on hand. Once it is heated, it is ready to serve. I usually top it with croutons. On a warm night, when soup would not be a huge hit, I go with a cold pasta salad, which takes a lot less time to whip up than you might imagine. As the pasta boils, I cut the veggies and drain the tuna. Then I rinse the noodles in cold water, pat them dry, and mix them together with either mayonnaise or an oil-and-vinegar dressing. I can make either of these dishes in less time than it would take the pizza delivery person to arrive and ring my doorbell.

Ultimate Shopping List Strategies

Now that you know which ingredients you'll need to prepare the next two weeks' worth of meals, you have to make a shopping list. Along with the ingredients that you'll need for your menus, you'll have to buy a few other items. Check your fridge and pantry to see what's missing or running low. Now that they are organized, it will be easy to see what you have on hand and avoid buying things you don't need. Organize your shopping list by categories or by aisle, so that your shopping experience will be more orderly. Then you won't have to run around the store to pick up items that you accidentally passed by. It's always frustrating to get to the checkout line or, worse yet, back home only to remember that you forgot the milk. Make some photocopies of the master list. You can then either circle items as you compose your shopping list or slip a list in a clear sheet protector and use a dry-erase marker to check off what you need. Always keep your list in the same handy spot, such as on the kitchen wall or inside a kitchen cabinet door. If you are electronically inclined, keeping your list on your phone or PDA might work for you.

More and more grocery stores are offering an online shopping option. Although this takes a little bit of time to set up, in the long run it saves you both time and money. If you don't want to do this for all of your items, consider it for some of the larger things that can be a pain to carry through the store, such as diapers, toilet paper, paper towels, bottled water, and so on.

Grocery Shopping Secrets

Simply reading the scanner as the cashier rings up your items can save you hundreds of dollars a year. Just last week I caught a mistake on the scanner at checkout. The cashier rang up my bananas as organic, when they were just plain old yellow bananas, a whopping $2.74 mistake! Who knew?

Always look for proper codes; for example, in produce inexpensive parsley can be mistaken for pricey cilantro. Also confirm the cashier has keyed in the proper quantities. He or she might count a dozen sesame seed buns in your bag, when you only chose ten from the bakery bin; a difference that can cost you a dollar or even two. The sensitive scanners can sometimes double-ring an item, and you also want to be sure that your coupons are credited properly. On average, scanners overcharge on one out of every ten items that are rung up. It might simply be a result of an item's price not being updated in the store's database, so watch for mistakes and speak up.

You couldn't pass up the sale on spaghetti squash? Okay, fine, but before it spoils, find a recipe that incorporates the squash and write it on the calendar.

The average American family of four spends about $107 a week on groceries, according to the Food Marketing Institute, and we toss out 15 percent of the food we buy.

Would you like an extra $100 or more in your pocket every month? Get ready to save *big* on your grocery bill. Try these tricky tips for super savings.

The early bird gets the deals. In most stores, shopping on a Thursday night means that you will be among the first shoppers to take advantage of sale items that, by the weekend, might be low or sold out.

Shop online for deeper discounts. Try buying your groceries online at your local store's site and have them delivered. You can even buy groceries from Amazon.com. Shop Tuesday through Thursday for the best deals.

Be a comparison shopper. Most stores will match a price, so if you see something advertised at another local store, clip out the ad and stop by your grocer's customer service desk. Your store will most likely match the price for you.

Shop for yourself and some friends. We've all heard of shopping in bulk. Sure, for certain things, such as your family's favorite cereal, it makes a lot of sense. But come on, who really needs twelve tubes of toothpaste? That supply would last for years to come; most likely, the tubes would expire by the time you could use them all up, and in the meantime you'd have to find room to store them. If you're a bulk shopper, be sure to read the unit price. Just because an item appears to be a good deal does not mean it really is. And find a friend, a neighbor, a coworker, or a family member who likes similar brands as you do and shop together. You can split the order and the cost, a win-win all around.

Dry food saves $5. No one wants to pay for water, but that's what you do when you purchase wet produce or icy seafood. Take a moment to dry your produce if it has just been sprayed with water; otherwise, it will weigh more and wind up costing you more money. Ask the employee to knock off any encrusted ice before packaging your seafood purchase.

Shop solo and save $5. Not only will you be in and out of the store faster, you won't be asked to buy extra items or treats to keep little ones quiet. If you must bring your children along, make sure they have something to do to keep them occupied.

Bend and save $10. The best bargains are closest to the floor, so get your exercise and bend down. And it won't come as a surprise when you find out that the most expensive items are placed at eye level, at the checkout, and right where kids can see (and beg for) them. Here's an insider's tip: cheaper items are always farthest to the right on the shelf, so keep walking down the aisle until you get to the end.

Evade end cap displays and save $20. Run, don't walk, away from items grouped together for convenience. Sure, they might look like a great deal, but when you see groupings for special occasions, such as cranberry jelly, stuffing, green beans, and French-fried onion rings, the grocer has placed them there in hopes that you'll scoop them all up on impulse. Many times, you do. Don't fall for this marketing trick. And check the aisle. Just because an item was moved to an end cap does not make it the cheapest option.

MONEY $ SAVER

Trying one or two of the fixes on pages 135–139 will save you, on average, $100 a week. Then, $100 a week put into savings at 5 percent interest will bank you close to $5,000 in just one year, nearly $27,000 in only five years, and a whopping $58,000 in ten years.

Full stomachs save $10. Shopping when you're hungry is a huge mistake. Everything looks good, and you end up buying all sorts of items that are not on your list. If you find yourself at the store and realize that you're hungry, you'd be better off buying a single-size snack and eating it while you shop. The extra money you spend on the food will be far less than the cost of all the impulse items you'd buy because you were starving.

Special items save $12. Paying for convenience can crush your budget. Medicine cabinet items, home-improvement tools, makeup, and even bread tend to cost more when purchased at the grocery store. An extra trip to pick up painkillers or your favorite lipstick at the pharmacy or a screwdriver from the home-improvement store or bakery items from an outlet store (see BakeryOutlets.com) pays off in a big way. Yet you don't always have time to get each item from a specialty store. I'll admit that I spent double the price by picking up a bath mat in the grocery store when I could have waited a day until I ran an errand to the home store. But that was offset by the dollar I paid at the grocery store for a money order for which my bank wanted to charge me $15!

Shop local and save $30. If you've never stopped by your local farmers' market, you don't know what you're missing: local produce and other foods grown near your hometown for sale at very reasonable prices. Because the items do not need to be shipped, buying locally saves your cash and the planet.

Reconsider at the conveyor belt and save $5. Just because you put it into your cart does not mean you have to buy it. As you empty your cart onto the conveyor belt, look over your items and don't feel shy about telling the cashier that you've changed your mind about an item or two.

Stock up after the holiday and save $20. Do you know the best time to buy hot dogs? The week after Memorial Day. How about when to stock up on corned beef? The week following Saint Patrick's Day, of course.

Pass up precut and save $5. Precut, prewashed food might save you a little time, but it spoils a lot faster and costs at least 20 percent more. Most of the time, the monetary savings outweigh the time savings, so go for the food that you have to wash yourself.

Choose frozen, not fresh, and save $25. Fresh fish from the seafood counter has almost always been previously frozen, so read the signs and consider buying the less expensive, still-frozen seafood. And give frozen veggies and fruits a try; they are picked fresh and flash frozen so they keep much longer than produce from the produce aisle. Don't overlook frozen herbs either.

Buy big and freeze, or cook double and save $32. If you have room in your freezer to store food, it makes sense to buy in bulk. You can purchase bulk quantities of meat and other items, repackage them in smaller portions, and freeze them yourself at home. Another way to save time and money is to cook double portions of meals that freeze well, such as soups and casseroles or lasagna.

Avoid individual servings and save $9. Sure, they're cute, all of those little cups of individual servings of cereal and soup, but are they 75 percent cuter? I doubt it. Once you find out that you could buy four regular sizes for the price of just one convenience size, they lose a lot of their appeal.

Get to know your store and save $20. Ask whether your store offers double days or accepts two for the same products. Ask for a price match and find out which "buy one, get one" sales require you to actually buy two. Lots of times, you can pick up one and save the same amount per item.

Limited numbers save $40. When something is limited in number, you can purchase it because the price is close to the wholesale price, so scoop it up.

Making friends in the grocery store. Most shoppers rush in and rush out, never acknowledging the store's hardworking employees. Not only is it nice to pay attention to these people, but it can save you money. My grocer's bakery cake decorator, Emily, has offered me samples. I've asked for and gotten smaller sizes of packaged meat. I even swing by the customer service desk to see Jackie and Pete, and they direct me to good deals and new inventory and have gone out of their way to apply coupons to save me the most money. Leo in produce has gone to the back and personally picked me the best mangoes and apples of the bunch. And Kevin lets me in on little-known secrets and helpful information, such as the time of day that the store marks down items in the bakery, the seafood, and the meat departments and what will be on sale next week.

Once you master some of the basic meal planning, coupon clipping, and grocery shopping routines in this chapter, you can start keeping a price book. This is a simple little spiral notebook in which you jot down what you generally pay for certain items. That way, you'll know when something is a good deal.

Clip and Collect Coupons

Clipping coupons does not happen in your spare time. You need a routine, just as with any other organizing project. Clipping on a Sunday is preferred, because that is when most of the best coupons for the next week come out. You risk missing a great deal if you procrastinate. The Sunday newspaper is not the only place to come across coupons you can use. Choose one or two other ways to bring in more coupons. Keep in mind that you don't want to get flooded with so many coupons that you feel overwhelmed and stop clipping them altogether. Clipping no coupons is not great, clipping some is very good, and clipping too many is a recipe for disaster.

- E-mailed coupons: sign up for coupons with your local grocery store and the manufacturers of some of your favorite brands of food. Instead of clogging up your every-day e-mail inbox, sign up for a separate free e-mail account for the sole purpose of accumulating coupons.

- Get two copies of the newspaper or ask a non–coupon clipping friend or neighbor to save you the flyers.

- Print coupons from online at places such as SmartSource .com, Valpak.com, CoolSavings.com, Coupons.com, and MyGroceryDeals.com; search Google for "coupon code + the name of the store or item."

- Many times, coupons are printed directly on your store receipt, so be sure to check it. Don't forget the coupons that print out at the checkout register and the ones found throughout the store in self-dispensing machines near the actual product.

- Always check the product when you're buying it. Sometimes it will have a peel-away coupon that is valid right then.

Clip coupons only for brands and products you use. No matter how good the deal is on cat food, if you don't own a cat, then there's no sense in clipping the coupon. The same is true with laundry detergent; if you see a good deal on a brand you haven't used, it may turn out to be one you don't like, and you may waste time in the store looking for it. Stick to the familiar; you know where your favorite brand is, you know that it works, and you know you'll like it. Group coupons in one of those coupon files according to store aisle: frozen foods, cookies/crackers, medicine cabinet, and paper products.

Are you unsure how your grocery store is laid out? Ask for a store diagram at the customer service desk or check the store's online Web site and print the diagram. As you put new coupons into your purse/car/file, weed out the expired ones. There's no need to recycle all of those expired coupons; instead, support our troops by sending to the Overseas Coupon Program, which collects old coupons and distributes them to U.S. military bases around the world. Coupons can be used up to two months *after* their expiration date; pick a base to support at OCPnet.org/base_list.htm.

When you make up your shopping list, write the letter "C" next to items that you have a coupon for. Designate a single canvas bag as your shopping tote where you keep your coupons, various store discount loyalty tags, and other canvas bags to take with you grocery shopping. Hang the bag on a hook near the front door so that you can grab it on your way out to the store.

When Not to Redeem a Coupon

- If the coupon is not good at your regular store. When you have to drive out of your way or shop in an unfamiliar store, you may waste more time and gas than it is worth.

- When you compare the cost per ounce and the nonsale item comes out cheaper, such as when buying a multi-pack or a larger box.

- If you are not sure of the brand or the quality or whether you will use it in a timely manner.

- If you already have too many of that item at home.

- If you are simply picking up an item to get the extra sale bonus, such as the free hand cream that comes with purchasing a certain shampoo with a coupon.

- If the coupon is for a specific size or quantity that does not make sense for you.

Is clipping coupons really not your thing? Delegate the job to a family member, such as a teen or someone else who likes to clip, and offer him or her a portion of the money you saved as a bonus. You could also trade the job for another chore that you'd prefer to take on.

How to Organize Your Recipes

Although it would be nice to have all of those clipped and printed recipes neatly organized, that is a longer-term project. For meal-planning purposes, you simply need a handful of recipes to get started. You can always go back and organize the piles later. There are two basic ways to organize recipes: one is on index cards and the other is in a binder system, using clear plastic sheet protectors.

Work in small blocks of time, using whichever system you choose. For the binder system, slip the recipes into the clear plastic sheet protectors; this is an easy way to go because you can see the whole recipe if it is double-sided. If you opt for index cards, you will need to cut the recipes down or possibly rewrite them.

Choose one night of the week to try a new recipe from your collection to find out whether it's a dud or a new family favorite. If it's a keeper, take the time to organize it, but never take the time to organize a recipe until you've tested it.

File the recipes by categories: for example, chicken, appetizer, slow cooker or soup, salad, and casserole. You can even go so far as to make categories for times of the year, such as BBQ and holidays. There's no sense in wasting time flipping through all of your cupcake recipes just to find the one recipe that describes how to make a spider web cupcake. It's better to keep similar recipes together and create a Halloween category.

Managing Your Takeout Menus

Sometimes it's inevitable that you will order out. Hopefully, this will happen less often than in the past, but there will be days when you're just going to phone it in. The good news is that because you've saved so much money in the kitchen, you'll more than cover the cost of a takeout meal or two (or three) and still have money to spare.

Gather all of the takeout menus that you have collected, and slip them into a single folder. Recycle any menus that have outdated prices or that you don't order from anymore. Then clip any coupons you have to the correct menu so that you have a better chance of remembering to use them the next time you place an order.

It is a good idea to copy the phone numbers from the menus into your cell phone's phonebook or keep a list in the glove compartment, because you might find it easier to order while you are on the way home, instead of waiting until you get home. This will save you time and gas, because you can pick up the food on your way home instead of making a second trip. When you enter the numbers into your phone, place the letter "R" in front of every entry so that in the alphabetical contact list, all of the restaurants will be grouped together. You might also find it helpful to keep a folder with duplicates of the menus and stash it in your car in case you want to place an order but need to look at the menu.

Now you've got all of the information you need about meal planning. You've learned how to set up your calendar, control your recipes, make a simple shopping list, and keep your takeout menus in order.

But the problem is trying to keep it organized. How can you use these solutions for the rest of your life? Remember, everything doesn't have to be perfect. So, maybe one day you will start to make a certain recipe and find that you're missing the carrots. Use a green pepper instead, if you have one on hand, or skip it altogether. Just because you won't be following the recipe exactly doesn't mean that it won't taste good. And if you're willing to experiment a little, you might be surprised by the delicious recipes you cook up on your own.

If something comes up one night and you won't be able to make the meal you planned, it's not the end of the world. Everyone encounters problems, and no one is perfect.

So, get over your fear of becoming organized because starting is the hardest part. Dive in, try your best, and if something doesn't work right away, don't give up.

The Zen Way to De-Clutter Your Closet

A Wardrobe That Suits You, Here and Now

How often do you say to yourself, "I have nothing to wear"? Logically, you'd think this comes from not having enough articles of clothing, when in fact the exact opposite is true. You have too much, and you can't find a thing. No, I'm not kidding. It's a fact, and here's why: when you have too much, your closets, dressers, and laundry are too cluttered for you to put an outfit together. Not to mention everything that might be packed away, tucked under the bed, or suffocating in space bags.

How did you get to this point? Mostly, from buying more and not paring down. Some of us may fluctuate in weight and therefore hold on to a wide variety of clothing sizes. You may have accumulated partial outfits from the sale rack or

MONEY SAVER

When the seasons change, *stop* the habit of buying an outfit or two to get you through until you drag out your stored clothing. When you pack up seasonal clothing, leave out an outfit or two that you can use when the seasons change again. If you live in a climate with cold winters, make sure that any wool outfits you leave out during the summer are protected against moth damage, in sealed plastic bags or tightly zippered plastic clothing bags.

abandoned items from friends and family members who knew you'd give the clothes a good home, even though these items should have been recycled. Or maybe you have a bunch of clothes that used to be right for your lifestyle, such as high-end designer suits for a corporate job. The only trouble is, you've been working from home for the last seven years. Today is the day to bring your unused clothes out of your closet and put an end to the "I have nothing to wear" dilemma once and for all.

Maximize Your Wardrobe

You don't need to shop for new clothes. Chances are, you already have them. It's time to attack your cluttered closet.

Start by weeding out the clothes you definitely don't need, and then make another pass through the remaining outfits that require more careful consideration. Have a fashion show. Keep the stuff you use and love, and toss the moneymakers into your sellables box. Make a note of anything that needs to be replaced or repaired.

If you have space in your storage area, use a wardrobe moving box to store out-of-season hanging clothing; the clothes can hang without getting wrinkled. Get one for free by posting a wanted ad on Freecycle, or go to U-Haul's box exchange.

Pay per Play

Before I list all of the essential items of clothing that a well-prepared and never-out-of-fashion woman needs to survive in modern life, I'd like to tell you a little cautionary tale from my past. It perfectly illustrates the difference between needing and desiring something. Sometimes we fall in love with an object and feel that we absolutely *must* have it. Powerful emotions make us want the item so intensely, we believe that just owning it will change our lives. Yet we usually find that the afterglow of the purchase disappears rather quickly, and our lives continue as they were—except for the fact that our closets and our houses are now crammed with too many temporarily lusted after possessions. Why is this?

A long time ago my mother taught me how to calculate an item's true value. I can remember wanting to spend my

MONEY   SAVER

When packing clothes for storage, reuse the silica gel packets that came in the plastic bag when you purchased bedding or in the box when you bought shoes. Meant to absorb excess moisture and most odors, these handy little gems are expensive to buy but free if you use the ones you get with a purchase. Just use caution, as silica gel is harmful if ingested by people or pets.

allowance on a pair of shiny silver pants. It was the 1980s, what can I say? She didn't say no; she simply asked me how many times I envisioned myself wearing them, before they went out of style. Because these were not the kind of pants one could wear after they were no longer fashionable, I guessed about five times. "Okay," she said, "and how much do they cost?" "Thirty dollars," I told her. "So then you'll be spending six dollars each time you wear them," she said. She then asked me a great question: were they worth six dollars a wear? When she put it that way, the pants became much less appealing. In case you're wondering, I left those pants on the rack and ended up spending only $3 on another trend, stretchy neon bracelets that at $3 worn every day for even just a month equaled 10 cents for every wear.

The Twenty-Two Things That Do Belong in Your Closet

1. Black pants
2. Black pumps
3. Black suit
4. Black turtleneck
5. Black wrap
6. Cardigan
7. Crewneck sweater
8. Cropped jacket
9. Denim jacket
10. Great-fitting jeans
11. Khakis (To get a perfect fit, have them made just for you by LandsEnd.com, which like L. L. Bean offers a lifetime guarantee to replace or repair clothing for the life of the item—no kidding!)
12. Little black dress

13. Long-sleeved T-shirts (black, white, and a flattering color for your skin tone)

14. Pencil skirt

15. Perfect-fitting T-shirts (black, white, and a flattering color for your skin tone)

16. Sneakers

17. Sweats or yoga pants

18. Tanks (black, white, and a flattering color for your skin tone)

19. Tote bag

20. Trench coat

21. White button-down shirt (This beauty is a classic piece that can be reworked into a variety of looks, such as layered under a suit, worn under a T-shirt or a cardigan, and worn open over a T-shirt or simply alone.)

22. Zippered hoodie

The things that *don't* belong in your closet are articles of clothing that:

- Don't fit you today
- Don't make you feel great
- Are from your past
- Are for your future

Keep in mind that your goal is to pare down your possessions by half, then reuse half of what you have, saving yourself a trip to the shopping mall. With a bit of creative thinking, you can maximize what you have. A little tailoring can go a long way. I can honestly say, I would not know where to begin to turn a pair of hole-in-the-knee jeans into a denim skirt, but I know it can be done. Often, taking a garment to a local tailor or bartering tailoring with a talented friend will save you lots of money in the long run. Just ask. Dresses can be turned into skirts or tops, long sleeves with worn-out cuffs can be cut down into three-quarter-length sleeves, and too tight or too loose clothing can be made just your size.

- Rethink uses for the clothing you have; think like a stylist (or barter with a stylist friend).
- Dye the garment to make it work—make a bridesmaid's dress into something you'd wear again.
- Turn a knee-length coat into a cropped jacket.
- Use a blouse as a swimsuit cover-up.
- Turn a miniskirt into a full-length skirt by adding a band of trim.
- Taper wide-leg or boot-cut pants.
- Turn a collared shirt into a mandarin-collar one.
- Turn a cardigan into a short-sleeved sweater.
- Turn a cocktail dress into a formal top.
- Make a summer dress into a skirt.
- Turn an ankle-length skirt into a knee-length dress.
- Make a sundress into a skirt.
- Make a pantsuit into a safari suit.
- Dress up almost anything and make it look new with embellishments.

Even without a tailor, you can rework your wardrobe:

- Accessorize.
- Let things move into other seasons—a T-shirt under a blazer works in the winter.
- Wear a vest over a button-down shirt.
- Wear a long skirt as a dress.
- Wear a spring dress over a long-sleeved T-shirt and leggings.

- Add a belt.
- Use boots to create a different look.
- Throw on a jacket.
- Wear a T-shirt under an open button-down shirt.
- Give shoes a whole new look with shoe clips.

Closet Clutter Busters

Use a large lidded basket to store out-of-season clothing; it can also function as a bedside table.

Screw drawer pulls into wall studs to hang purses, jewelry, or the jeans you'll wear again this week.

Hang towel racks on the wall, on the back of a door, or in the closet to hold jewelry.

Attach a cookie-cooling rack to the wall to store jewelry.

Rolled magazines will stop boots from creasing by keeping them upright.

CD cases can house necklaces tangle-free and ready to travel.

Bubble wrap makes a great travel pillow.

Stuff a pair of pantyhose into a paper towel tube. You can label what color or style they are, they pack better, and you won't snag them in the dresser drawer.

An ice cube tray works great as an earring organizer.

Laundry Myths That Cost Us Cash

1. Clothes shrink in the dryer. Actually, not so much; in fact, most clothes shrink while being washed in hot water. The solution is to wash them in cold water. This saves your clothes and your hot water bill.

2. Socks are lost in the dryer. This doesn't happen very often, although some socks cling to other clothing during the drying process. Most socks are lost in the washer. Because they are so light, they float to the top and spill right over the drum and end up wrapped around the motor. With the sock mystery solved, save your washing machine and stop replacing socks by clipping a matched pair together with a clothespin before washing them, or wash them in a lingerie bag.

Shoe Mania

No one wins by leaving this earth with the most pairs of shoes, I promise—and you can't take them with you. You have only two feet. Even if you wear two pairs of shoes a day in one month, the most you'll need is sixty pairs. So, dare I ask how many shoes are in your closet or under your bed? I'll go out on a limb and say you do *not* wear all of the shoes you own. The Consumer Reports Research Center states that women own an average of nineteen pairs of shoes. I'm guessing that their husbands were within earshot when they answered that question, because I've been in closets all across America, and most of them contain way more than nineteen pairs.

Of the fifty pairs of shoes that most of us own, we wear only about ten. The rest are too pretty or too painful to wear. If you love shoes, then you might want to sit down before you read this: you only need only five pairs of shoes. Start breathing again, it'll be okay. Just hear me out.

The Shoes You Need
1. Black pumps
2. Boots
3. Flats
4. Sandals
5. Sneakers

The Shoes You Want

- High-heeled boots
- Brown pumps
- Flip-flops
- Sexy shoes in multiple colors and styles
- Snow/rain boots
- Trendy (and cheap) shoes
- Trendy (and cheap) sneakers

With your shoes relegated to the dark depths of the closet floor under all of those hanging garments, it's really no wonder that you don't know what you own or can't find a matching pair. Shoes that you love go unused, a few pairs become your everyday shoes, and you buy more that look eerily similar to ones you already own. The shoe quandary is a major one. But it is a big problem with a little fix. Ready for this? Get your shoes off the floor. And no, you don't have to get expensive custom racks to display them or photograph each pair to stick their photo on the front of the box.

A slim-line floor-to-ceiling bookcase is the very best way to display those shoes. Pare down your collection by half, and display the rest of them on the bookcase. It is too difficult to locate the other pairs in the black hole of your closet floor. Based on the size of your closet, you may have to finish build-ing it *inside* the closet, or you just might not fit it in. Yes, I speak from experience. When storing shoes, alternate them on the shelf or in the container to save space.

Avoid Buying Endless Variations of Purses, Bags, Totes, and Clutches

I'll admit that bags are my weakness, much more than shoes. I love the possibilities. I'll see a bag in the store and imagine all of the things I could put inside it, places I could carry it,

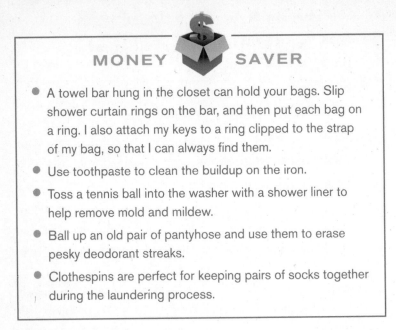

MONEY SAVER

- A towel bar hung in the closet can hold your bags. Slip shower curtain rings on the bar, and then put each bag on a ring. I also attach my keys to a ring clipped to the strap of my bag, so that I can always find them.
- Use toothpaste to clean the buildup on the iron.
- Toss a tennis ball into the washer with a shower liner to help remove mold and mildew.
- Ball up an old pair of pantyhose and use them to erase pesky deodorant streaks.
- Clothespins are perfect for keeping pairs of socks together during the laundering process.

and the adventures I could have. It's silly, I know, but true nonetheless. Over the years, I've been able to whittle down my collection, and I am much more thoughtful about new purchases. For example, I know that I need an outside pocket; it's the place I slip my car keys into. Without it, I'm lost. So now, if I'm looking at bags, I cross all the ones without an outside pocket right off my list. The thing is, most bags are the same. Whenever I bring a new bag home, I usually find an almost identical one already in my closet.

Knowing what purses, bags, totes, and clutches you already own makes it easier to remember what, if any, style or shape you are missing. As with shoes, classic is always better because it can serve a wider variety of purposes. Store your purses in a way that you can not only see but also get to the one you want. As we all know, if we can't find the one we own or don't see those that we own, we are much more likely to buy another.

How to Have a Custom Closet on an Off-the-Rack Budget

Save your money and the environment by opting to create your own custom closet. The best part is that because it is not built in, you can change it or move it any time your needs change. Doesn't this sound perfect? Here is how you can create your own tailor-made closet for a fraction of the cost.

Materials to have on hand:

- A slim-line floor-to-ceiling bookcase (or two)
- Shoeboxes in a variety of sizes
- Wrapping paper in a color or pattern you love
- Baskets—square or rectangular shapes with lids are best
- Large-size white address labels
- A double hang bar
- A stick-up light
- Hooks
- A marker

1. Build a slim-line floor-to-ceiling bookcase in your closet to display your shoes. If you are not an "I love to put clothes on hangers" kind of person, you may want to add a second bookcase for stacking folded clothes instead of facing the dreaded clothes hanger.

2. Stash small items like scarves and belts in shoeboxes. For a clean, high-end look, take a moment to wrap the boxes in your favorite wrapping paper so that all of your boxes match and you cover distracting logos. Use the address labels to label each box so that you know what goes where.

3. Baskets are a great storage option for a wide variety of items. Out-of-season clothing can be stored in a large basket with a lid. A smaller basket can hold accessories and a medium-sized one can hold sweaters or T-shirts. Mixing wrapped boxes and baskets gives your closet a nice look. Sitting them on shelves or stacking them on the floor works well.

4. You can instantly double the amount of hanging space in your closet with a double hang bar, which slips easily over the rod that's already installed in your closet. If your closet is tall enough, you can also hang out-of-season clothing up high by installing a rod a few inches below the ceiling and using a reacher hook to pull garments down as needed or rotate them for the season.

5. Hooks are some of my favorite organizing tools because of their versatility. Depending on the size of the hook, you can hang anything from handbags to belts, to hats, to your everyday jeans.

6. Hang an over-the-door shoe holder to avoid wasting the space on the back of the closet door. Although it's not always ideal for holding shoes, it is a perfect storage solution for socks, accessories, and so much more.

7. Hang a battery-powered stick-up light so that you can see your outfits more clearly. It seems like the last thing that closets in multimillion-dollar homes have is lighting. It is such an overlooked feature but is one of the most necessary. No more dressing in black pants and navy shoes!

Find Savings in Every Room of Your Home

Avoid Sneaky Clutter-Cash Traps

Aside from offices, kitchens, and closets, other areas in your home can cost you money. I'll describe the main money drains and provide doable solutions within the framework of the half-and-half method. Implementing these remedies today to plug the money leaks means more money. Imagine having more money—in most cases, *a lot* more—back in your pocket starting tomorrow! You may be surprised to discover some of the sneaky ways that being disorganized hits you in your pocketbook. Stop putting it off. Reclaim your cash by jumping in and cleaning up your clutter, while you find even more treasures to sell.

Keep an eye out for these moneymakers: artwork, china, heirlooms, collectibles, holiday decorations, out-of-season or outgrown clothing, paintings, and flatware. And don't forget items that are stored with family members or friends.

Where have you lost money? Do you rebuy items that you know you already have but simply can't find? Have you ever tried to return an item to a store without the receipt only to find out you won't get the full credit? And how many of you have paid rush charges to mail a gift to someone, maybe at the holidays, because you procrastinated about getting it in the mail? Have you ever been penalized for misplacing important documents?

First Impressions: Is Your Entryway Organized or Overflowing?

The entryway of your home seems innocent enough, but in reality it's one of the biggest money pits in the house. Consider the wildly overstuffed hall closet, all of the clutter that accumulates in the entrance, such as shoes and backpacks, and those everyday life essentials like a cell phone and bills to be mailed. An entryway makeover can instantly put money back in your pocket.

I'd like to tell you about my foolproof plan for saving you money by getting rid of entryway clutter. I've worked with many clients to transform their hall closets into makeshift mudrooms. Are you interested in that idea? Start by blocking off about an hour, then pull everything out of the closet. Let go of jackets that fit no one, and recycle wire coat hangers that are too flimsy to ever hold a heavy winter coat. Box up excess hangers, which will be perfect for displaying sale items. Then hang a clear-pocket, over-the-door shoe holder on the inside of the hall closet door or on the wall, if you don't mind how it looks—and you might not, because many of these organizers come in decorator's colors and patterns. Remember, these solutions are best placed by the door that you use most often.

Do not place shoes in the pockets of the organizer; instead, use them for life's accessories, such as cell phones (and their cords), dog leashes, and sunglasses, plus all of those items you don't want to forget on your way out the door, like outgoing mail and library books and DVDs of movies to return. You can even use one pocket for receipts and another for kids' car toys. Once you have a home for everything you need to grab as you head out the door, you will notice a big difference right away. There will be no more forgotten bills that need to be mailed and no more lost cell phone charger cords that cost $20 to replace; plus, your receipts will all be in one place in case you need to return something you bought.

Take advantage of wasted space by taming that unruly hall closet. You have little to no hope of wrestling out a coat hanger to hang up a jacket. Most of us would be hard-pressed to even name everything that is in our hall closets. Often, many of those items can be relocated to another area of the house, freeing up valuable space where you need it the most.

While you're organizing, here are some moneymakers you may come across: seasonal accessories, such as gloves, jackets, and shoes, and sporting equipment. Don't overlook pet accessories. The cute hoodie your dog wore last winter might be too small now, but it can be sold for a pretty penny. Look for dog training cages, travel crates, clothing (including holiday costumes), and anything else you and your dog no longer use. Don't forget your other pets while you're at it; hamster wheels, fish tanks or filters, and even bird cages can be sold for profit.

Next, hang a good battery-operated light so that you can see into the rest of the closet. You will put in a bench and shoeboxes and will install hooks for hanging things, such as backpacks and jackets. Depending on the size and shape of your closet, you might even fit in a slim-line floor-to-ceiling bookshelf for more storage space. Put back the items you use

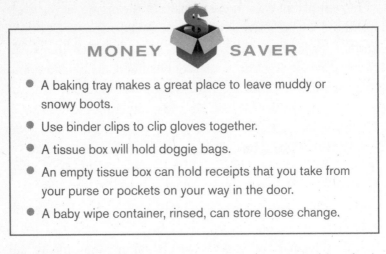

MONEY   SAVER

- A baking tray makes a great place to leave muddy or snowy boots.
- Use binder clips to clip gloves together.
- A tissue box will hold doggie bags.
- An empty tissue box can hold receipts that you take from your purse or pockets on your way in the door.
- A baby wipe container, rinsed, can store loose change.

frequently, such as hats and gloves; then store everything that's left elsewhere in the house. Reworking a closet can really go a long way toward helping you stay clutter-free.

Do you want to clean less often? I sure do! The answer is, don't allow outdoor shoes inside. The fewer shoes that make it into your home, the less dirt you'll have to clean, which saves you time and money on cleaning supplies or hiring professional cleaners. A simple large basket by the front door is a perfect depository for shoes. If you like to wear shoes in the house, keep an indoor pair here and make the switch. Then use one basket or container per family member for his or her items. This keeps everything organized, and when the basket overflows, it's time to put some items away. This simple technique will keep accessories off the floor and separate for each person, so that less time will be spent searching for lost or misplaced items.

How to Have Pleasant (Clutter-Free) Dreams

Why is it that a relatively small space beside the bed can turn into such a big mess? Between the towering stack of books (mostly unread), a teetering pile of mail, a bunch of bills (still to be paid, no doubt), and a troublesome number of photo frames, not to mention all of the little items such as tissues, hand cream, and television remote controls, it's no wonder you can't get a restful night's sleep.

Take everything off your bedside table, and clean it well— yes, even the lampshade, by gently using your vacuum cleaner or roll a lint roller over it. Now put back your reading light and alarm clock. If you are cramped for space, opt for a wall-mounted light. If you tend to hit the snooze button one too many times, move the alarm clock across the room so that you are forced to get out of bed. The worst alarm I ever invested in was one that went into snooze mode if I even waved my hand from three feet away; there was no need to touch a button. I was late for almost everything that year!

Now, place everything else on the floor next to your bed. If you don't reach for one of those items before you wake up the next morning, chances are you don't need it as often as you thought. It makes more sense to store it elsewhere. For example, take those magazines. Some are moneymakers, such as the cooking or specialty ones; consider selling them. I prefer a nightstand with a shelf or, even better, a drawer. You can tuck things away and keep the space that you see clutter-free. If you don't have a shelf or a drawer, no worries. You can slide a basket underneath, which will work just as well.

Keep your bedside work-free. You don't want nonstop access to a BlackBerry chock full of work e-mails or a cell phone with voice mails; it makes for anything but a relaxing time. Put a pen and a notepad nearby to jot down to-dos as you think of them, so that you don't try to remember everything in your head, which would prevent you from falling asleep. And that treadmill you're using as a towel rack? It's another big moneymaker; think about selling it and hanging your towels on a hook.

Your Bathroom: Stop Flushing Money Down the Drain

I'll bet you'll be surprised to learn how much money can be found in the bathroom. It's not a big room, but it's a big budget buster. There's the linen closet, the medicine cabinet, and don't even get me started about the area under the sink. Replacing just one lost lipstick can set you back $12.

Are you ready to make money by giving your bathroom a fresh start? Here's what to do. To begin, make money every time you flush your toilet by adding a plastic soda bottle filled with water to the tank. This will trick the float mechanism into thinking that the tank is full, thus using less water with every flush. Ka-ching.

Now, on to the medicine cabinet. Stop rebuying medications that you already own or misplacing the tweezers, which forces you to pony up another four bucks to replace them (only to find the original ones in a drawer the same day). If you have time, pull everything out of the medicine cabinet. If not, work in eighteen-minute blocks of time and do each area in order. Wipe the shelves down, and put back only the *unexpired* items that you actually use frequently. The rule of thumb is that you must use them at least weekly. Try organizing them according to your daily regimens. Place everything you use while getting ready in the morning on one shelf; it will be easier to find, and you are less likely to skip a step in your beauty and health routine.

No more overbuying. When you have a linen closet where you can actually see what you own, you won't waste money buying things you don't need. So, if the towels stacked in the linen closets bear an unfortunate resemblance to the Leaning Tower of Pisa, you need to organize. Toiletries and towels are expensive; buying more because the ones you own are hidden costs money.

Put money back in your pocket by rearranging your linen closet. First, remove everything and wipe down the shelves. Next, put back the items you use and *only* the items you use. I'm not kidding. *Do not* put back sheet sets for mattress sizes that you no longer own. And seriously, no one needs twelve beach towels! Slip matching items for sheet sets inside their pillowcases, and keep a maximum of three for each mattress that you currently own. Now, take out your bath towels. You need only three per family member. Make a stack of your cleaning rags. After that, it's all about the toiletries and the paper products. Group similar items together, keep the most frequently used items at eye level, and put seasonal linens on the upper or lower shelves.

Unopened makeup and spa products and hair appliances such as flatirons are all big moneymakers.

Now it's time to go into the dark depths—yes, under the sink. (Of course, if you have a pedestal sink, you are excused from this section.) Until someone comes up with a solution for getting those pesky pipes out of the way, you'll have to work around them. Yet it might not be as difficult as you think. Once you have the space cleared out, you need to put the items back in such a way that you can find what you need when you need it. Stacking containers with lids work nicely, as long as you label them. The few moments that it will take to get out the container you need is nothing compared to the mishmash of clutter that accumulates when there are no storage containers under the sink.

Insider Bathroom Tips

- Hooks are inexpensive and can tame the mess of towels and robes. Because they can be hung at varying heights, they're great for short and tall people alike. The new

Command hooks by 3M can even be removed in one piece without leaving a sticky residue. And the largest size holds up to sixty pounds!

- Use baby food containers for beauty products such as bath salts.

- Put a basket in the bathroom for towels, toiletries, or spare toilet paper rolls.

- Use one basket per person, containing items he or she needs to get ready in the morning.

- A berry basket or egg carton can contain makeup or hair accessories on the vanity or in a drawer.

- A spice rack can hold pill bottles or spa products.

- Use a wine rack to hold towels or reading material.

- Utensil drawer organizers work for makeup in the bathroom drawer.

- Toothbrush caddies work as makeup holders.

- A full tissue box can function as a manicure station; slip a bottle of nail polish where the tissues pop up to hold the bottle secure.

- You can toss expired items and share free makeup samples that you know you'll never use. If teal blue eye shadow or plum lipstick is not you, find someone whom those shades flatter. Don't overlook your local community playhouse. I'll bet teal eye shadow looks great onstage; it's just not that appropriate when you pick kids up from soccer practice.

- Regarding all of those sample or travel sizes of lotions, shampoos, and so on, of course I'd prefer that you save money and bottle your own as needed. But instead of wasting the ones you already have, group them together so that you can pick what you need for sleepovers or vacations.

Your Purse or Wallet: Stop Carrying Extra Weight

KRISTEN'S STORY

Kristen was driving home from work when a police officer pulled her over. It turned out that the inspection sticker on her car had expired six months earlier. The officer asked for her driver's license and insurance card. Little did he know what a challenge that would be for Kristen. After rummaging through her purse, she finally just dumped it out on the front seat. A pen, makeup, tissues (some used), gum, receipts for the last few months of shopping in case she needed to return anything (such as the cole slaw her family had already consumed at a picnic), and so much more, spilled all over her car. When she could not locate the card in her wallet or purse, she tore apart the glove box. Finally, Kristen came across a few insurance cards, but on closer inspection she realized that they had all expired.

Why am I keeping expired cards? she wondered. In the clutter explosion, she was able to put her hands on her license but found no insurance card. The officer was forced to write her a traffic ticket. When he handed her the $120 ticket, he also gave her some advice. "Kristen," he said, "you have to get organized!" No truer words had ever been spoken. After this $120 ticket, Kristen decided that she could not afford to be disorganized any longer, and she vowed to clean up her act, starting with her purse.

Like Kristen I saved money by lightening my load in the purse and wallet areas, and you can too. First, I took an extra key ring and grouped those store loyalty cards together; now they don't clutter up my wallet and key chain. Next, I pared the contents of my wallet down by half, putting back only what I use. I keep my extra credit cards safe at home. I carry an envelope in my bag so that I can put receipts in the envelope, instead of jamming them into my wallet. I also use an old tin from breath mints for my business cards and a few scraps of paper. I even found a tiny pen that fits inside the tin.

Now I can see what I have and find it when I need it. Plus, I won't be holding up the line at the store while I dig around for something. If your wallet could be just a little more organized, try to tackle your purse this week. It doesn't take as long as you think; in fact, you could do it while sitting in a waiting room or in a car waiting for your child to come out of school.

Did you know that the average woman's handbag weighs three and a half pounds and has sixty-seven things inside?

Essentials

- Money
- ATM card (Use a rubber band to wrap a note around the card, with a reminder question written on the paper: "Is this absolutely necessary?" This will prevent impulse buys.)
- ID
- Keys
- Sunglasses
- Reading glasses
- Compact
- Lipstick
- PDA/calendar
- Cell phone

Designing Your Craft Room

A well-organized craft room can be an inspiring refuge. If you store all of your supplies in this one location, it's so much easier to keep track of materials you have on hand and those you need to replace. If you don't have an entire room that you can dedicate to crafting, even the corner of a room can be set up as a work space. The essential thing is that you have a flat working surface, a comfortable chair, good lighting, and ample storage for your supplies.

While sorting through your craft room, remember that you can sell completed craft projects, as well as craft supplies, so box up the ones you are not using. Don't forget gift wrap, gift bags, and other wrapping materials, which also have great resale value.

Here are some tips to help you organize your work space:

- Use an aluminum pie plate to corral project pieces as you craft.

- Use an egg carton to store little bits and pieces and craft items.

- Use a baby food jar to store small items, such as buttons, safety pins, and snaps.

- Use a wine rack to store rolls of gift wrap.

- Paper towel cardboard insert tubes, when slit longways, make a cuff to prevent an open roll of gift wrap from unraveling.

- Pizza boxes, large and unused, can store scrapbooking materials and other craft supplies.

- Paper towel holders—the wooden kind with the dowels—can be used to slip on rolls of ribbon for crafting or gift wrapping.

- Spice racks can store craft glitter.

- Toothbrush caddies can hold craft items such as paintbrushes.

- A dish rack works as a craft caddy.

- Use a berry basket as a paintbrush organizer; simply place the basket upside down on your crafting table and insert the paintbrushes, handles down.

- Baby wipe containers can store buttons and spare lengths of thread from clothing.

Book, Movie, and Music Madness

Have you ever stepped on a DVD? If so, you know that number one, it hurts, and two, it doesn't take much to crack one to the point of no repair. That's about $15 down the drain and another $15 to replace it. Media centers in your home come complete with CDs, DVDs, video games, gaming consoles, gaming magazines (with important game codes), and more wires than you can count. Not to mention the countless cases— empty, of course, because everyone seems incapable of returning the disc to the case. This means you are losing money, hand over fist.

You can really cash in on your media and craft areas. Be on the lookout for big moneymakers, such as books of all genres; electronics—cell phones, cameras, and stereo equipment; video games, gaming devices, and accessories; music; and don't overlook the movie collection.

Once you've pared down your media room by half, it's time to organize. Let's start with the empty cases. You may simply have to accept that the discs are not going to make it back into their cases. Instead, create a CD book or a wall hanging for them. At a glance, you will then be able to find the CD you are looking for. It is much easier than opening all those cases, because sometimes a DVD was put away in the wrong case or got scratched so that it skips at the best part of the movie.

Cord ties work well to gather and hold the bird's nest of wires; if you label the plug end, all the better. Then you'll need a place to store all of the consoles and the manuals. An ottoman with a lift top for storage works well. Or a basket that you can slide under the coffee or side table.

Which brings us to the tower of media equipment: stereo components, DVD player, TV, and so on. Leaving them piled high overheats them and shortens their life span. Let them breathe.

Now that you've organized, you and your family may want to discuss new household rules about how media areas should be cared for so that you can all enjoy the room to its fullest potential.

MONEY SAVER

- A trunk can function as a coffee or side table and offers storage inside.
- A small chest of drawers works as a side table.
- A tissue box can store CDs or video games.
- A cake decorator's icing tip can hold a small stack of CDs without scratching them.
- A small hair clip keeps cords from getting impossibly tangled.

Clear Away Car Clutter

Seriously, the car can be a dangerous disaster zone. Think food wrappers, canvas shopping bags, expired coupons, random toys, sporting equipment (in and out of season), overdue library books, stray shoes, and backpacks. We spend a lot of time in our cars, yet we tend to overlook organizing this area, which ends up costing us money. Simply forgetting to bring your canvas shopping bags into the store and having to buy more at a few dollars each will cut into your bank account, plus you'll have even more bags to store and organize when you get them home.

You would never want a rolling object to get stuck under the brake while you're driving. You also don't want clutter sliding off the car seats to distract you. And when you can't find what you need, such as a snack or a diaper, you'll have to stop at a store and buy more. Not to mention that heavier cars use more gas, so a set of golf clubs stashed in the trunk wastes fuel. Just by taking a few simple steps, however, you can clear away the car chaos and save yourself big bucks.

Start with the glove box. Most of them are fairly roomy, but we stuff them full of items that we rarely use, such as the car manual, instead of items we need close at hand. Pop a zipper-lock bag with small first-aid items like Neosporin and bandages into your glove box. If you love the beach, keep a paintbrush there as well, to easily brush sand off your feet. The less dirt there is in the car, the less you have to spend on cleaning the inside. Slip an over-the-seat organizer on the back of the front seat to keep children's toys, media items, cords, maps, umbrellas, gloves, and other essentials at hand.

Speaking of kids, before you install a child's car seat or booster seat, spread out a towel or a sheet on the backseat so that it can catch the inevitable crumbs that will collect beneath your child. Let's not forget the trunk: a box or a milk crate will

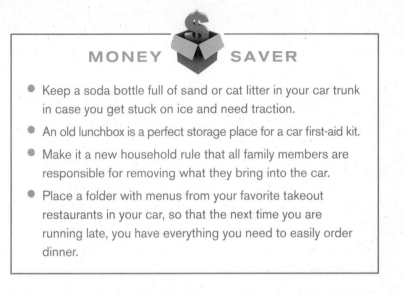

MONEY   SAVER

- Keep a soda bottle full of sand or cat litter in your car trunk in case you get stuck on ice and need traction.
- An old lunchbox is a perfect storage place for a car first-aid kit.
- Make it a new household rule that all family members are responsible for removing what they bring into the car.
- Place a folder with menus from your favorite takeout restaurants in your car, so that the next time you are running late, you have everything you need to easily order dinner.

keep bags from tipping over. Once a green pepper rolled out of my grocery bag. I spent a long time looking for it, and when I finally found it weeks later—well, let's just say that no one could have identified it as a pepper.

And try this new rule: every time you get gas, toss the trash.

Make Room in the Garage for Your Car

Let's face it, most people use their garages for storage, sometimes to the extent of not having enough space inside for their cars. But you can do both. The trick is to store garden, workshop, and automotive tools compactly against the walls, on shelves, and on hooks, and leave the center area for your car.

Moneymakers that might be hiding in your garage include camping and sporting equipment, extra auto parts (and automobiles), bicycles, automotive tools, lawn and garden tools and equipment, seasonal decorations, home repair equipment, ladders, luggage, and outdoor furniture.

Here are some tips to help you organize your garden, automotive, and workshop supplies:

- Use a Rolodex to store seed packets; staple them to the tabs alphabetically.

- CDs are great reflectors; when hung in the garden, they keep deer away. Or attach them to stakes to act as reflectors along your driveway.

- Egg cartons work for starting seedlings. They will also hold workshop items, such as screws and nails.

- Use a berry basket to protect seedlings from wild animals or from being stepped on. It also works as a screwdriver organizer in the garage. Attach the basket to the workshop wall (upside down or right side up—it doesn't matter) and insert screwdrivers through the holes.

- Use baby food containers to hold screws, nails, and nuts and bolts in the workshop area.

- A dab of toothpaste will fill in a nail hole.

- Prevent a padlock from rusting by slipping a tennis ball over it.

- A soda bottle top makes a perfect funnel for filling the car with fluids.

- Milk jugs can hold nails in the workshop.

- Toilet paper cardboard insert tubes make great cord organizers; they can store all of those extension cords that are always tangled up. Fold an extension cord back and forth, making it about ten inches long, and stuff into the tube. Use a marker to write the cord's length or what it attaches to on the tube.

- Pizza boxes, large and unused, are perfect to store holiday decorations.

Teach Your Kids to Organize Their Rooms

Stop those all-day toy pickup fests! The good news is that you can have your Saturdays back. Not only will you be able to enjoy your weekends again, but you'll save a bunch of money, too.

The secret to this newfound freedom lies in teaching your kids how to organize their toys and possessions. If you turn it into a game, they may actually have fun keeping their rooms in shape. And once they experience the benefits of being organized, it might motivate them to extend these organizing skills into other areas of their lives, now and in the future.

In a child's room, when the toy area is a mess, certain toys are not played with because they can't be found. Other toys get broken or pieces go missing, which costs you money. Or maybe your children have so many toys, they cannot even focus on, or have time for, all of their toys. It becomes sensory overload, resulting in a lack of appreciation for these items. Instead of buying multitudes of toys, perhaps you should put more money into savings or your child's college account and encourage other family members to do the same. Really, how many Lego sets or Barbie dolls can one child enjoy?

Pare down the contents of your kids' rooms by half, and then work to organize what is left. Opt for open storage bins whenever possible. Lids make it difficult to put things away. You know yourself that it's easier simply to put something down where it doesn't belong than to spend time popping off a lid to put it away in a box. The same is true for children. Rolling storage bins are a huge time saver, and kids tend to like them. They can roll the toys to any spot where they'll play with them, then roll them away when they are finished playing. At least, that's how it is supposed to go.

You and your child can add labels to the bins, or make it an art project by drawing a picture of what belongs inside. Or you can take a photo and use that. When everyone knows what goes where, it's much easier for kids to clean up their own rooms. Stuffed toys are always a challenge, though. They take up so much space, but they're so cute. (You already know how I feel about cute.)

As you organize, don't overlook the moneymakers inside your child's room, such as toys, games, collectibles, stuffed animals, premiums that came with fast-food meals, clothing, shoes, accessories, and toys you yourself owned but passed down to your kids.

Instead of letting arts and craft kits or other projects that need adult help go to waste, make a list. That way, you can refer to the list on a rainy day or when you're going to be out, and a babysitter can do a project with the children. Any toy that has lots of little pieces or requires adult supervision is best kept on a top shelf. No one wants to have to pick up 250 little foam stickers. The last important thing to do to save money in the play area is to designate a "missing parts container." If you find a stray puzzle piece or some Monopoly money, you can toss it into the missing parts bin and eventually match the parts up, instead of getting rid of toys with missing parts. Plus, if you end up giving away or selling the toy, having all of the pieces is a bonus.

If your child does not want to pare down his toys by half, try these three techniques:

1. Offer to sell the items and split the money, giving him some for spending and putting the rest into savings.

2. Explain there are children who do not have any toys, and let him bag up a specific number of toys to share. Then bring your child with you to a shelter or other charitable organization so he can see where the toys are going.

3. Box up some toys and tuck them away for a rainy day. When your child complains about being bored, you can pull out the box of forgotten toys and swap it for a bunch of other toys he has not been using.

MONEY SAVER

- Hang a basket on the wall or place it on the bookshelf for odd-size books.
- Use over-the-door shoe holders with clear pockets to store small toys. If they are hung low enough, this storage option even works for toddlers. Dolls, accessories, cars, and so much more can fit easily inside the pockets. The best part is that, at a glance, your child can find what he or she is looking for.
- Pizza boxes, large and unused, are great for storing children's artwork or memorabilia.
- Toothbrush caddies will keep items together that kids need for homework, such as rulers and pencils.
- Egg cartons can hold kids' treasures, such as rocks and shells or small toys and their accessories.

Turn Clutter into Cash

How to Maximize Your Profits, Selling Online and in Person

You've done the hardest part: you've pared down your possessions by half and boxed up lots of stuff to sell. Now you have those five full boxes, and you can't leave them sitting in the corner gathering dust. That stray sweater, a tiny toy, a seldom-used salad spinner, and that bunch of books will earn you a lot of cash, but only if you actually sell them.

Good news—I've taken all the guesswork out of the process. I'll give you some insider tips from my years of experience on how to sell your stuff for the biggest profits and what pitfalls to avoid. This chapter will cover the ins and outs of determining what to sell, where, and how. I'll also reveal my advice for saving time. This is a chapter that you'll refer to over and over again for years to come. Are you wondering what that sound is? It's the sound of cash going back in your pocket!

Yard sales and popular online auction sites are not the only ways to turn your cash into clutter. To prevent you from getting overwhelmed by the choices and spending hours researching where to sell your various items, I've laid out the pros and cons of a wide variety of options, along with information on where each item is most likely to fetch big bucks. Here are the venues you have for selling your stuff:

- Yard sales
- Online auctions
- In-person auctions
- Flea markets
- Online stores
- Classified ads
- Consignment shops

Trash or Treasure? Make Sure before You Ditch It

To be honest, if you showed me four porcelain figurines and asked me to pick out the Hummel, I'd have only a 25 percent chance of getting it right because I really have no idea what one looks like up close. I can't tell the difference between vintage and antique, and I am clueless about whether a Beatles vinyl album is worth something. So, how can you tell whether an item is worth a lot of money?

Not so long ago, the only way to know an object's value was to spend hours poring over price guides in the reference section of the library, but now there are quick and easy ways to accurately determine what an item is worth. Although reference librarians are among my most favorite people on the planet and working with them is still a great choice, there are other ways to track down the information you need, especially when the library is closed. One way that is *not* recommended is taking the item into the same type of shop that would buy such an item. I'm sure many of these shops are reputable and would offer an unbiased opinion, but you can't be 100 percent certain.

Sentimental value and current market value can be two totally different numbers. Although you may imagine that the quilt your grandmother labored over would sell for $2,000, you might be surprised to learn that unless Betsy Ross sewed a stitch or two, it does not have a high market value. Now sentimental value, that's a whole other story. These high or low numbers can be shocking. You might have been saving a base-ball card, thinking it would increase in value and sell for enough money for you to buy a vacation home, only to be disappointed at the price it fetched. On the other hand, you may have been ready to toss a figurine, then found out that someone just paid $100 for one just like it. One common misconception is that collections such as china plates, baseball cards, a Holiday Village, vinyl records, or *TV Guides* are automatically worth thousands of dollars. This is not so—sorry. Here are the top three reasons why your collection may not be worth all that you think it should be.

1. **It's too common.** Just because it was given a number or signed does not make it special. If the market is flooded with a large quantity of these items, they're not worth a lot. That Snuggie you couldn't resist ordering from a late-night infomercial, even sealed in its original package, is worth a little less than you paid for it, and if you don't have the free book light that came with it, forget about breaking even.

2. **It's too personalized.** You might not think so, but buyers find personalization less valuable. Although an auto-graph signed to your uncle is great, a simple signature is far greater.

3. **It's too damaged.** To an untrained eye, it might be impossible to detect subtle imperfections that occurred to an item in storage. But deterioration happens. Collections that are not kept in cool and dry places risk damage due to exposure to sunlight, moisture, and temperature fluctuations.

Remember, your collection is worth only what someone else wants to pay you for it. Sadly, value is not determined by how much we think it is worth; otherwise, we'd all be multibillionaires! To appraise your item, start by turning on the computer. These days, you can find the answer to almost any question on the Internet. Of course, you want the most reliable answers, so head over to eBay.com. Log on and search for the item you own. You'll come up with active listings (items that are still available to buy), which help you determine current interest in the item, as well as any closed listings (the item is no longer available to buy because it either sold or the auction ended before the item sold), where you can see what the item *actually* sold for, if it sold. To look exclusively at past listings, after searching for the item whose price you want to find, click on "Completed listings," and you can see what this item has sold for in the past on eBay. Another online searchable price guide that is supereasy to use is PriceMiner.com.

A good old-fashioned online search can yield a bounty of results, such as message boards and specialty collectors' sites. The key is to find the information you need as efficiently and as quickly as possible. Although it might be nice to chat on a message board or look up the values for items you don't even own, remember your goal. Think of it like this: you want to be paid a high hourly rate. Let's say that you sell a set of china for $200, and it took you two hours to research and list it; thus, you made $100 a hour. But if it took you four hours of research time, plus two hours to list it, you made only about $33 an hour. That's still nice, but you can increase your bottom line by staying on task. This means, whatever you do, stop yourself *before* you start bidding on eBay auctions!

Besides books and the Internet, another tool in your valuation tool chest is the phone. Simply text the name of the item and the word *price* to Google (466453), and you'll receive a text back with the current listings online for that item. It will take only a few minutes, and you'll have your answer for free. Rather, the service is free; you'll simply pay standard text-messaging rates.

Another option is to text the KGB at 542542 with a question, such as, "How much would my 1970 Limited Edition Holiday Barbie sell for?" Within minutes, you'll receive a very thorough answer. Let the KGB agent do the work for you, for only a 50 cent charge. Because the agents work twenty-four hours a day, seven days a week, you can receive answers even if you can't get on the computer and the library is closed.

Are you still having trouble finding a price? It may be worthwhile to hire an appraiser. You'll want to ensure that you work with an independent appraiser who has no interest in purchasing the items you are having appraised. That way, you will avoid lowball appraisals in the event that this person wants to buy the item from you at a fraction of its true worth. Independent appraisers usually charge somewhere between $150 and $300 an hour. You can get references for appraisers from organizations such as the Appraisers Association of America at Appraisers.org or AppraisersAssoc.org. Items like baseball cards, coins, dolls, and quilts have their own specialty appraisers' organizations, so search for your category and the word *appraiser* to find the specific association.

Before you shell out cash to hire an appraiser, check with your local library and community center to see if they are hosting their own version of *Antiques Roadshow*. You might get lucky. The library one town over from me hosts an antiques appraisal at least once a year. That's how I found out how much the child-size diamond ring I was given as a baby is worth. Yes, I am keeping it, in case you're wondering. My first pair of shoes were not worth very much, though. Want to make your treasure famous? Go to PBS.org and apply to be on the real *Antiques Roadshow* that airs on your local public broadcasting station.

Selling in Your Pajamas: Where to Sell an Item Online

Selling an item online can be through a "buy it now," a "best offer," or an auction, depending on which Web site you choose. The "buy it now" option means you put it up for sale and someone can buy it for the price you listed. Some stores offer a "best offer" option, in which case you sell it to the buyer who offers you the best price. The other option is an auction; you can put a reserve price on the item, which means bidders have to reach a minimum amount before it will sell. Then bidders continue to bid until the auction ends, and the highest bidder wins the auction and gets to buy your item. The most popular sites also happen to be the ones that get the most traffic, bettering your chances of a sale. These are eBay.com, AllMarket.com, Sell.com, Amazon.com, Facebook.com, Kijiji.com, Oodle.com, Bonanzle.com, and Craigslist.org. A little later in this chapter, I'll explain the pros and cons of each so that you can make the best choice.

Here's a step-by-step guide to a red-hot listing a bidder or a buyer is sure to notice:

1. **Appraise.** Appraise your item so that you know what you've got and how much to charge.

2. **Account.** Open an account and buy a few small things to get a positive rating so that people feel more comfortable buying from you. When you create an account, be sure to use a name that sounds professional. Although a shop named IHeartButterflies is cute, it may not instill as much confidence in a buyer or make you as easy to find as Jill's Sporting Equipment.

3. **Price.** Price your item about 10 percent above where you want to end up. Most items sell for about 10 percent less than this list price. Bump up the price a little and offer free shipping and handling or a small free gift with the purchase. Buyers *love* free stuff. Around holiday time, offer free gift wrapping to really make your listing stand out. The only caveat here is that if you're shipping something very heavy, such as computer equipment, and you offer free shipping and you factor this expense into your item's ultimate price, a Web site like eBay will end up taking a bigger percentage of your profits than if you hadn't offered free shipping. This is because eBay takes its final fee as a percentage of the total price when the item is sold. If your total price is $100, but if paying for "free shipping" costs you $35, then eBay will take a percentage of the $100, rather than a cut of the $65 that is your true profit.

4. **Reserve.** Consider using a reserve price. These listings usually cost more, so unless you really can't part with it for less than a certain price, don't choose to list a reserve price. This option is available only if you are listing your item for auction. Don't forget to state your return or exchange policy, if any, and whether you charge restocking fees for returned items. This is also where you can suggest that the buyer pay an additional fee for shipping insurance.

5. **Photographs.** Photograph your item in way that really shows it off. There's no need to create elaborate backdrops; in fact, the cleaner the background, the better. That way, the shopper can focus on the item without getting distracted. Clean up the item and get it camera ready. Wipe off any dust or fingerprints, and make sure it is wrinkle-free, then take a picture of the item. Take snapshots from multiple angles and some close-ups as well. You may not use all of the photos in the ad, but if a shopper requests more photos, you'll have them to send. Make sure to get pictures of the inside and the outside of items such as tote bags, and if there are labels or tags, snap a shot of those as well. If there is any related paperwork or if you have the original sales receipt handy, get a shot of that, too. Remember, no one wants to buy a crumpled skirt that is photographed spread out on your dirty floor. Iron or at least smooth out the skirt, then hang it for the photo shoot. The final sale price should make it worth your while.

6. **Measure.** Measure the item so that you'll be able to give an accurate description. On a handbag, measure the width, the depth, the height, and the shoulder drop. Count the number of pockets inside and out. All of these details can mean the difference between a sale and no sale, or a sale for a little or a lot of money.

7. **Describe.** Describe the item using evocative phrases. Are you stuck for another word for *great* or *smooth* or *red*? Use a thesaurus, like the one at Thesaurus.com. Using descriptive terms will increase your sales dramatically. Honestly, which would you rather buy: a "brown sofa" or a "luxuriously supple leather sectional in a highly sought-after coffee color with a heavenly reclining chair and compartments galore for storage"?

8. **Headline.** Give your ad a headline that says what the item is, because those are some of the main keywords that will be used when someone is searching for it. This is not the place to get cute or fancy; doing so will only hurt your sales. Think like the buyer. If you were looking to buy the item that you are selling, what words would you type in?

9. **Buzz.** Spread the word about the item you have for sale by adding a link to your online sale in the signature line of your e-mail, tweet about it on Twitter, and write it on your wall in Facebook.

10. **End.** End your auction (if you are listing it on an auction site) at a time when you can take advantage of last-minute bidders. If your auction ends at four in the morning on a Tuesday, most of your bidders will be sleeping. If your auction ends on a weekend, however, your bidders are more likely to be online watching your item and continuing to bid.

11. **Payment options.** Paypal is the online money exchange system currently owned by eBay that allows you to get paid. So you'll definitely need an account with Paypal if you are listing your item on eBay. Even if you are not using eBay, you still might want a Paypal account because you can use it to collect money from other sites. Paypal does charge a nominal fee for processing transactions, but since Paypal does all the work, it's worth it. I've used Paypal with confidence for years and never had a negative experience. If you are unfamiliar with online accounts, though, you might feel uncomfortable setting up your account because you have to give Paypal your bank account information so that it can send you your money. Remember, you can always open a

bank account that you'll use specifically for this purpose, so that at any given time Paypal would have access
only to an account with a zero or minimal balance. Also
try Google Checkout, where you can open an account
and Google will collect payment on your behalf for less
than 3 percent of the transaction plus 30 cents.

12. **Store.** Store the item until the auction ends or until the
item sells. I can't tell you how nerve-wracking it is to list
an item and then promptly misplace it. Or worse yet, to
have something happen to it, forcing you to pull your
ad. Designate one place for all of the items you currently
have up for sale. If possible, make the storage area convenient because you may have to look at the item to answer
a buyer's question.

13. **E-mail.** E-mail is the only way a potential buyer has to
communicate with you, so it is *very* important that you
check yours regularly. You need to be on top of checking
incoming messages. Nothing kills a sale faster than failing
to promptly reply to a buyer's inquiry. The buyer figures
that if you don't e-mail a reply quickly, then, chances are,
you won't ship the item quickly either.

14. **Ship.** You need to ship the winner his or her purchase
as soon as possible. This ensures that you receive a good
review and builds confidence in future bidders. Not
getting the item out the door immediately results in a
negative seller rating. Consider using a tracking method
when shipping to confirm that the buyer received the
item, so that you can avoid anyone making fraudulent
claims that the item was never received.

15. **Feedback.** Just as you'll likely get feedback from the
buyer, you can leave feedback for the buyer, and it is
always a courteous thing to do.

ONLINE SELLING SITES

Selling Site	How It Works	What You Can Sell	What It Costs	Listing Length	Getting Your Money	Store Option	Rates Sellers and/or Buyers
Amazon.com	Log on and key in the ISBN number. When the item pops up, click "Have one to sell," and it walks you through the listing process, including suggesting a sales price.	Books, CDs, DVDs (or just about anything if you opt for the store option)	You are assessed a commission charge of 6–15% plus a $1 transaction fee and a variable closing fee.	60 days	Buyers pay Amazon directly and Amazon credits you for the shipping costs. You get an e-mail when your item sells. After the buyer confirms receiving the item you shipped, Amazon puts the money into your account.	For a monthly fee of $40, you can get a pro merchant account, where you can list items other than books, CDs, and DVDs, plus Amazon waives the $1 listing fee and the listings never expire.	Sellers
Bonanzle .com	You list a "Buy it now" ad, plus you can import items you have listed for sale on Craigslist and eBay.	Anything	Ads are free to list, with up to four photos. When the item sells, you pay between .50 and $10, depending on the final sales price.	Listings do not expire until they're sold or deleted.	Buyer pays for shipping, if there is any, because you can also list items for pickup.	None	Neither

Craigslist.org	Free classified ads.	Anything	Ads are free to post.	Listings do not expire.	Doesn't collect any money. You'll need a separate account to allow the buyer to pay you.	None	Neither
Ebay.com	Auction-style listing or a "Buy it now" option, allowing buyers to make the purchase without the bidding process.	Anything	First five listings per month have no insertion fees; beyond that a basic listing fee is up to $4 plus a percentage paid when the item is sold.	5–7 days		For a monthly fee of $16, you can get a virtual store, which gives you lower up-front costs and your listing will not expire.	Sellers and buyers
Facebook.com/marketplace	Free local classified ads.	Anything	Ads are free to post.	Listings do not expire.	Doesn't collect any money; you'll need a separate account to allow the buyer to pay you.	None	Neither
Kijiji.com	Free local classified ads.	Anything	Ads are free to post.	Listings do not expire until the item is sold or deleted.	Buyer and seller meet and exchange goods for money.	None	Neither

(continued)

ONLINE SELLING SITES (*continued*)

Selling Site	How It Works	What You Can Sell	What It Costs	Listing Length	Getting Your Money	Store Option	Rates Sellers and/or Buyers
Oodle.com (Facebook marketplace is powered by Oodle so only use one of them.)	Free local classified ads.	Anything	Ads are free to post.	Listings do not expire.	Doesn't collect any money; you'll need a separate account to allow the buyer to pay you.	None	Neither
Sell.com	Online classified ads.	Anything	Listing fees vary by item type, from free to $6, and you can add on additional features for more money, but there are no fees when the item sells.	30 days	Doesn't collect any money; you'll need a separate account to allow the buyer to pay you.	None	Neither
TalkMarket.com	Online video classified ads.	Items you create.	They take a 20% commission.	Listings do not expire.	Doesn't collect any money; you'll need a separate account to allow the buyer to pay you.	None	Neither

Besides the places in the chart, where you can sell almost anything and everything, you can locate groups of potential buyers on Meetup.com. For example, a meet-up group of photography buffs might be interested in your old photography equipment. And for a little more help, here's a list of places to sell specific items by category. Sometimes the name can be deceiving, so check the site to see what it accepts. For instance, TextbooksRUs.com will pay cash for more than simply textbooks, although you would not know that based on the name.

Appliances

ScrapSpot.com

RecycleInMe.com

Automobiles

eBay.com

Vehix.com

Books/Textbooks

AbeBooks.com

BetterWorld.com

CashforBooks.net

Chegg.com

Half.com

HalfPriceBooks.com

TextbooksRUs.com

CDs/DVDs/Records/Games

Amazon.com/tradeingames

CashforCDs.com

EBGames.com

Gamestop.com

Gazelle.com

TheCDExchange.com

SecondSpin.com

Spun.com/sell

Cell Phones/Computers/Cameras/Tech Stuff

CellforCash.com

FlipSwap.com

Gazelle.com

GreenPhone.com

SecondSpin.com

SimplySellular.com

Note: When selling computers and cell phones, remember to keep your personal information safe by deleting the voice mails and your contacts and resetting your password to 0000.

Electronics

TuneCycle.com

SmallDog.com

Furniture

FurnitureTrader.com

Gift Cards

CardAvenue.com

PlasticJungle.com

SwapaGift.com

Homemade Arts and Crafts and Crafting Supplies

Etsy.com

HomespunHeaven.com

Ink/Toner Cartridges

eCycleGroup.com

RecyclePlace.com

Jewelry

JewelryBoxMining.com

USGoldBuyers.com

Kids' Clothing/Toys

KidtoKid.com

Ouac.com

Laptops

CashforLaptops.com

Sporting and Exercise Equipment

PlayItAgainSports.com

Wedding Dresses

WeddingDressMarket.com

Sure Ways to Sink a Sale

Here are the top ten mistakes that sellers make. Avoid these costly errors, which can reduce your profit margin or sink your sale altogether.

1. Recover all of your item's pieces and parts. You don't have to launch an all-out rescue mission for an owner's manual or the extra baking rack that belongs with the toaster oven. But take a quick look; maybe you still have the owner's manual handy or the accessories that belong with the vacuum cleaner that you're listing for sale. These extra pieces make the item more sellable and that means more valuable.

2. Never use more than three capital letters in your listing's headline. Honestly, STOP screaming. A MUST-SEE

NEW IN BOX GREAT CONDITION 1960 BARBIE
YOU'LL LOVE HER is not nearly as appealing to read
as Must-See 1960 Barbie NIB. Not only are capitals difficult to read, they are just plain rude.

3. Don't overuse exclamation points in your description, as
in "True Tin Toy Collection!!!! Will love!!!! Check this
out!!!!" It's distracting to read and annoying; plus, it low-
ers your searchability, so fewer people will actually read
your ad.

4. Dollar signs only remind people that they will be spending money, and when we're shopping, who wants to
be reminded that we're parting with money? Which of
these looks better to you: $45.00 or 45? For a buyer, the
one without the dollar sign is more appealing.

5. Not describing the true condition sinks the current sale
and jeopardizes all future sales because once you have
bad feedback, your rating is damaged. You are already
unknown to the buyer, and no one wants to buy from
an unknown person with negative feedback. Your online
reputation is all you have. Do everything you can to make
sure it is a good one.

6. Give your item a reasonable price. If you have an unre-
alistic expectation of what your item will sell for, this is a
problem. If all the other striped tiger Ty Beanie Babies
are listed for $2 and you list yours for $30, you're not
going to make the sale. It doesn't matter why your pricing
is out of line: whether you are sentimentally attached or
simply want to see if you can make more money. Buyers
will catch on and skip your item.

7. The words in your title come up in buyers' searches, so
don't waste space with words such as *great buy* or *hot
item*. Instead, focus on what you are selling. Be sure to use

a few listing keywords (descriptive phrases) separated by commas, such as *pearls*, *brooch*, *pin*, and *jewelry*.

8. There is no way to time the market. If you wait to see whether the interest in your item will go higher, you risk losing a sale altogether. The right time to sell is when the scale tips from your wanting to store the item to wanting the freedom and the money that come from letting someone else pay you for it.

9. Don't forget to include your contact information. I can't believe I even have to say this, but ad after ad either has mistyped contact information or none at all. How, exactly, will potential buyers let you know they want to pay you?

10. Use spell check. Please. I know I'm not the only one who has misspelled a word or two, but typos are glaring errors in a short paragraph describing the item. Silly errors do not build confidence in buyers.

Insider Tips to Collect More RICHES

Relate to the buyer. Would your buyer call it a couch, a loveseat, or a sofa? Use each term as a keyword so that your listing will appear in your buyer's search.

Identify common typos. Check out TypoBuddy.com to see common misspellings, then use the misspellings in your listing so that your ad will come up in a buyer's search if he or she makes the common misspelling.

Cross-list the item. A pearl necklace could be listed under "jewelry" as well as under "crafts," so list it in both areas to double your buyer pool.

Host as if you're on QVC. Hosts for television shopping channels talk about a product using words that make you feel like you have to have it. They talk about limited quantities and the product's benefits, and they hype the item with very descriptive words. Instead of simply saying *pink*, use flowery words such as *fuchsia* or *petal pink*. Consult a thesaurus to find words that will make the item irresistible to a buyer.

Encourage visitors. You need people to read your ad. The more people who see what you are selling, the more buyers you'll have. It's a numbers game. So promote your ad on a blog, and link to it from a message board or a social media site you belong to, such as Facebook, MySpace, or Twitter.

Scope out competition. Search for the product you are selling on the online auction site. Focus on auctions that have the highest number of bidders, and pay attention to how these sellers set up their auctions, whether they use photos, how they describe the product, and how they priced the item.

Can Someone Sell This for Me?

I'm glad you asked. Sometimes selling an item is just not your thing. You may not be tech-savvy enough, have no free time to spare, or simply not be interested in doing this. But the profit from selling, well, that's interesting. You can opt to let someone else do the work and pay this person for his or her time or let the individual share in the profits. Who might this lucky person be, who can help you turn your clutter into cash? Start at home: do you have a child or a spouse who might be willing and interested enough to take on the task? Or might they do the job as a gift to you for your birthday? Instead of giving you more clutter, they could help you get rid of some. I've watched parents ask their teenage children to sell a thing or two, and in exchange they would get some of the money. You don't have a teen of your own? Find one. Does your friend or neighbor have a teenager? Instead of babysitting or doing yard work, he or she could hop online for you and collect the same average hourly rate. How about a niece or a nephew?

Hitting up friends and family is not the only way to get some help, though. You could leave your stuff at a store that specializes in selling on eBay. Keep in mind, however, that the store will take a hefty percentage, maybe even 20 percent or more. Still, if it is a choice between your not selling the item at all and making nothing or doing next to no work and making 80 percent—well, you do the math. I'd gladly take the 80 percent. Such places include 877ISoldIt.com (1-877-I-sold-it [476-5348]) or eBayTrading Assistant.com or AuctionItToday.com. New stores are popping up all the time, so check your local yellow pages.

Auction Houses

Unless you are an art or antique collector who buys objects in person at auctions, you may not even be aware of the auction houses right in your own neighborhood. These often overlooked opportunities are known for turning clutter into cash. You don't have to bring antiques or high-end collectibles; you'd be surprised at what bidders want. There's no need to feel intimidated. If you've never attended an auction, here's the inside scoop.

The most basic explanation of an auction is this: a bunch of people in a single place are interested in buying the same object, so they take turns bidding on the object, and the highest bidder is the one who gets to buy the item. Some auction houses have specialty or themed auction days; for example, toys or glassware. So keep an eye out for those, because the attendees on those days are *guaranteed* to be interested in the item you have for sale.

A big benefit of live, in-person auctions is that you can bring delicate or oversize items such as furniture that would be costly or difficult to ship. Nevertheless, there is no clear-cut way to tell where your item might fetch the most cash. Mostly, it depends on the time you want to invest. A live auction will not require you to take photographs, deal with shipping, send e-mails, or worry about processing payment from the winning bidder. In contrast, with an online auction, you can do everything from start to finish without ever leaving your home. To locate an auction house near you, check the yellow pages or search Google for "auction house + your zip code."

One final note about auction houses: if you are going to take some wares to have auctioned off, *do not* go with cash in your own pocket. Register as a seller *only* and not as a bidder so that you won't be tempted to buy anything. Your goal is to get things out of your home, not to bring new things in.

Most auction houses have general guidelines about what they accept, and many also have specialty auctions for specific types of items, so check with them before you drive your items over. Once you know what to bring and at what time, you'll take your items there and the auction officials will direct you as to which table to place them on. You'll probably get some sort of identifying sticker to mark your lot(s), which is what each item or group of items is called. If you have an item that you must get a minimum dollar amount for before you'll sell it, then you'll set a "reserve price," which means that this minimum figure needs to be met before the item can be sold.

You may also place a few items in a "box lot"; this simply means that related items such as glassware or records are placed in a box and sold as a single item. Box lots can drive up your profits because, chances are, there are multiple bidders who each want at least one of the items in the lot, so they bid against one another. If your lot sells, then you collect your money minus the auction house's commission, which is generally 10 to 20 percent. If your lot does not sell, you can take it back. Maybe you'll drop it off at a thrift store on your way home.

Some auction houses will offer to keep the unsold items for you. Whether to take them up on that is up to you. You may want to get the tax write-off or try to sell them at a later date. On the other hand, you may just want them out of your home and it might make sense to let someone else take care of it for you. If you know you'll be tempted not to sell the items after all, then you should definitely leave them at the auction house.

Consign for Cash

Consignment shops choose which products, designers, styles, and sizes they want to specialize in. Some may take almost anything of quality; others may deal only in children's clothing and toys; while others may be high-end stores with designer bags and name-brand labels. Once you locate a shop using the yellow pages or ConsignmentShops.com that matches what you have to consign, here's what will happen. You and the shop will enter into an agreement; basically, the shop agrees to do its best during a set period of time to sell your item(s) in exchange for a percentage of the selling price. Typically, you can expect the shop's percentage to run somewhere between 30 and 70 percent of the item's selling price, but remember, as with most things, this might be negotiable. Once your item is sold, the consignment shop takes out its fees and sends you a check for the difference.

Are you wondering what happens if your item does not sell? Your contract with the shop should spell that out. For example, you'll agree to consign the item for a specific period of time, usually somewhere between thirty and ninety days. If the item does not sell, you should have the option to pick up any unsold items or have them donated to a local thrift store. Be sure this option is stated in your agreement. Which is a better option? That depends. If you will be prompt in picking up the item and you'll drive it directly to a thrift store without being tempted to take it home with you, then opt for the pickup option and donate it yourself to get the tax benefit. If, however, you know you can't be trusted not to bring the item back home and you might be tempted to put off making the pickup, then it is best to let the shop handle the unsellables. Be honest with yourself. The potential tax benefit is not worth much if you waste time and money and end up bringing the item back home with you.

It is extremely important that you keep your receipt for consignment in a safe place, but not so safe that you forget where you put it. This is your only official record of the items you've left at the store. I paperclip mine to the calendar 30–90 days forward, which acts as a reminder, plus then I'll have it when I need it.

Yard Sale 101

Here's the deal with a yard sale. You are allowed to stockpile items to sell only if you are actually going to have a yard sale sometime during this century. I'm not kidding. I've seen really valuable items crammed into boxes to be sold "one day," but by the time the sale day comes, the stuff is ruined. Items in storage can be broken and crushed, the heat or humidity can ruin them, water damage can happen, and pests can get into the boxes. Last year I received an e-mail from someone who had been planning to have a yard sale, but when she opened the boxes of clothing, she saw that they had been shredded and made into nests by clever critters. Too bad. They were nice clothes, and she could have made lots of money by selling them. She really regretted not simply giving them away, rather than letting them be ruined. If you are ready to rake in the cash at your own yard sale, however, that's super. Here's how to have the most profitable yard sale ever:

- Multifamily sales get twice as much traffic as single-family ones. If you can pull off a group gig, do it. If not, just sell your own stuff.

- Some towns host yearly townwide sales. Check with your local municipal building to see whether you can join an upcoming one.

- Some towns have sales in places like train stations. You have to rent a table, but the added traffic might make it worth it, especially if you share the table with a friend or a neighbor.

- When choosing your sale date, avoid major holidays and choose a date near the 1st or 15th of the month, which is right around payday for most of your buyers.

- One-day-only events make more money. With weekend sales, people who miss day one don't come on day two because they assume that all of the good stuff is gone.

- If you place "guy stuff" such as golf clubs and tools near the curb, more people will stop, because men will see something for them to look at while their wives shop.

- Have a table with crayons and coloring pages for kids to keep busy while their parents shop.

- Create a basic sign that is weather-protected. It should have lots of white space and be clearly written, mentioning only a few big-ticket items. Using arrows is helpful.

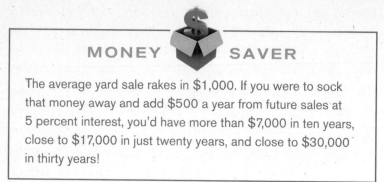

MONEY SAVER

The average yard sale rakes in $1,000. If you were to sock that money away and add $500 a year from future sales at 5 percent interest, you'd have more than $7,000 in ten years, close to $17,000 in just twenty years, and close to $30,000 in thirty years!

- Serve coffee, iced tea, or lemonade to keep shoppers around.

- Play music. Silence can make shoppers uncomfortable, and music makes them more likely to buy. Choose soft elevator music.

- If you plan to price items, opt for placing plain colored dots on the items. Then post a chart showing each colored dot and its corresponding price. That way, later in the day, you can slash prices easily by simply changing the price on the poster and not on each individual item.

Do you wonder which items you should concentrate your yard sale efforts on? The top five sellables are:

1. Furniture
2. Dishware
3. Kids' clothes
4. CDs
5. DVDs

Create a Buzz

To make big bucks, you need to have a big turnout. You have to get traffic to your sale, which means spreading the word.

Even if you are not a master of marketing, you can create a buzz for little to no cost. Signs tacked to telephone poles are still a good way to alert passing cars. Make your signs on yellow or bright pink poster board, which are the most effective sign colors. Remember, cars are driving by quickly, so you want the sign to be legible. Stop short of listing every single item you'll have for sale. Instead, draw an arrow directing the car to your location, write "FREE and sale items," give the date and the times, and maybe mention one or two of your big-draw items, such as a computer or a crib. That's it. If the sign is too busy, you'll defeat the purpose because people will have no idea where to go.

Don't let your efforts get washed away in the rain. Waterproof the sign by slipping it in a clear bag and taping it up or covering it in clear wrap. You could put an expensive ad in the classified section of your local newspaper, but that is not always the most effective way to publicize yard sales. Fewer people are reading newspapers these days, the ad space is small, and the price tag is high. It makes more sense to put an ad in the paper if you are having a multifamily sale because you can divide the ad's cost among the group members.

Online notices are a great way to go. You can list your sale on sites such as WeekendTreasure.com, GarageSaleHunter.com, Gsalr.com, YardSaleSearch.com, YardHopper.com, USGarageSales.com, GarageSaleSource.com, Craigslist.org, Myspace.com, Twitter.com, and Facebook.com.

And good old-fashioned flyers still work. Just concentrate your efforts on your target market. If you have lots of baby equipment, then tack flyers in the lobbies of local pediatricians' offices or tell mothers' groups. If you have some exercise equipment, then tell local gyms about your sale. Posting the flyers on local bulletin boards, for example, at the local grocery store, is always a great way to draw attention. And on the day of sale, put a sign on the front lawn to let people know you are actually having a sale and not merely cleaning out the garage. Although I have to mention that I was once working with a client to organize her garage. A passing car stopped and the driver asked to buy the crib and the stroller. We pulled together an impromptu sale, and my client made enough to cover the cost of her organizing project.

A Pricing Guide

Are you wondering what price sticker to put on your old mixing bowl or never-opened Scrabble game? Most likely, you'll be chewed down by about 25 percent during the haggling stage, so set the right price about 25 percent *above* where you want to end up, and display a sign that says "Negotiable," because everyone loves to get a bargain.

Here is a cheat sheet of what you can expect to get for common yard sale items:

Appliances/electronics: one third of their original price

Hardcover books: $1

Paperback books: 50 cents

Common vinyl record albums: $1

Instead of pricing each item individually, save time and group similar items together; then price the whole section. For example, on a table with books place a single sign: "All hardcovers $1, and everything else 50 cents."

It really is worth your time to put clothes on hangers. I know you can barely muster up the energy to hang your own clothes, but you might be more enthusiastic about whipping out those hangers when I tell you that clothes will sell for *four times* as much when they're on hangers. Here's another insider tip: items lying on a lawn blanket or in the driveway sell for only about a third of the amount of those displayed up high on tables. This is proof positive that it makes sense to drag out those folding tables. You can borrow tables from the neighbors or get creative and hang items from a clothesline. Even stuffed toys clipped to the line can look cute, and here's a bonus: they'll catch the attention of children who are passing by, which means the kids will drag their paying parents with them.

Remember, shoppers love freebies. Play to the shoppers' weakness by picking out a bunch of things that you never want to see again and placing them in a box labeled "Free." Shoppers and browsers alike can pick out what they want from the box, and everyone wins. This is a great marketing technique. With a "free" box near the curb, passers-by can see it and are much more likely to stop.

If you're not interested in the free box idea, go for a "gift with purchase" table instead. For every $25 spent, let the buyer pick an item, or you can wrap some of them up as a "surprise gift" with purchase and let the buyer choose.

Transform your yard into a high-end store by staging your items. For example, group a dress and a handbag with a necklace and add a sign that reads "Perfect for an evening out!" You could place a picnic basket with a fishing pole and make a sign that reads "Gone fishin'!" You could wrap two board games together with a ribbon and add a sign that reads "Family game night!" Taking an extra moment to make these little groupings will really pay off. They'll fly off the table!

Always bundle up the deals. Tie three books together; the buyer will pay for all three, even if he or she wants only one. When bundling, use odd price points so that it is not glaringly obvious how much an individual book costs. A bundle of three books for $5 or three videotapes for $2—you get the idea.

Your Timeline and Checklist

At least two weeks before the yard sale:

- Collect all of your goods.

- Start to stockpile boxes for display, and borrow tables from neighbors if needed.

- Check whether your town requires a permit, because some do.

- Start to get the word out.

One week before the event:

- Schedule an unsellables pickup with a local charity, or be sure you'll have a car for a drop-off.

- Gather a bunch of bags for purchases to have on hand (clean out your gift bag collection).

- Grab newspapers from your recycling bin to wrap delicate items.

- Flip through your owner's manuals to see whether you have any that go along with items you are selling.

One day before:

- Set up the sale. The more you can set up ahead of time, the better.

- Get change from the bank for your cash box.

- Put out a yard sign and signs on telephone poles, and add balloons to the signs (optional).

- Buy treats, coffee, cups, and lemonade (optional); use mugs that you're going to sell to give drinks away in for free.

The day of the sale:

Prep

- Make coffee or lemonade, and put out treats.

- Hang clothing on a rope between trees.

Set Up

- Set up a full-length mirror near the clothing.
- Wipe down plastic items to make them shine.
- Tape owner's manuals to sellables.
- Set up a kids' table with crayons and coloring books or free toys.
- Keep a tape measure handy for customers to check dimensions.
- Stage your sellables with "guy" stuff closer to the curb, and make sets with other similar items.

Last Touches

- Plug in an extension cord so that customers can check whether electronics or appliances are in working order.
- Have batteries on hand.
- Have your money container set up, keep the bills on yourself, and keep the change in an egg carton or a muffin tin.
- Turn on music to make shoppers more comfortable.
- Smile and have a super sale.

Breakdown

- Take down the signs.
- Await a pickup from a charity or drop off any unsold items.

Flea Markets

A flea market, sometimes called a rummage sale or swap meet, is like a huge yard sale, where a bunch of vendors gather to sell items. You can rent a table from the flea market organizers. Table rental fees vary from $10 to more than $100, depending on the venue. Although you would have to drive items to and from the market, the good news is that attendance is usually very high, so you have a great chance to sell lots of stuff. Plus, some markets are in covered areas, so you don't run the risk of getting rained out. Preparing for and setting up a flea market table is simliar to a yard sale, so you can use that checklist. You can find local listings at FleaMarketListings.com.

Classified Ads (Online and Newspaper)

Check with your local newspaper for ad prices. My hometown paper offers *free* classified ads to anyone who has something to sell, provided that the item(s) will be sold for less than $100. How cool is that? Contact the classified ad department and inquire. The newspaper may have limits on the length of the ad, and you'll want to know where to send it and what the deadline is for your ad to be run in next week's paper. If you are selling the item for more than $100 or your local paper does not have the free option, you can pay for ad space. Sometimes the fees are negotiable, so it never hurts to ask.

When writing your ad, start with a catchy title printed in bold text. You have only two seconds to catch the reader's eye and get him or her to keep reading. The title *must* say what you're selling. Don't be too cute—say what it is, plain and simple. An eye-catching title would be something like "1972 Mustang Fastback" or "Cherry Wood BR Set." Once you've settled on a title, you need the text. Once again, keep it short and simple. Shy away from uncommon abbreviations or any shorthand that only you would understand. Most readers will recognize 4 DR as meaning "four doors." But RWS could mean so many things, no one could possibly guess you're referring to a red-and-white-striped tote bag. Remember, even though you are paying by the word, if you chop up the ad so much that no one can read it, you're wasting all your money.

Do not forget your contact information. I'm not kidding. Right now, I'm looking at two nice ads:

> 35 in. Toshiba TV. Dual tuner PIP. 14 yr old tube set. Still has good pix. Buyer p/u $50 or b/o.

> MAYTAG APPLIANCES '01 (light almond set of 4) Original cost approx. $3500 make offer set/4 Fridge, Stove/Oven, Micro, & Dishwshr!

Let's say that I wanted a TV or an oven, I'd have no clue whom to contact. The owners spent money on these ads, and they are not getting a single response. In your ad, please provide your contact information. You'll want to do two things to double-check your accuracy. If you are giving out your phone number, you'll be surprised how many times you've typed it wrong but overlooked the typo while proofreading it. To catch this simple error, pick up the phone and dial the number. It'll just take a moment, and it is worth your time to avoid listing a wrong number. And if you are going to give an e-mail address, consider opening a second free e-mail account to use just for the duration of the ad. Sure, you'll have to check two e-mail accounts for a little while, but you'll be glad you did. First, you'll avoid ad inquiries cluttering up your everyday e-mail inbox, and second, you'll protect your personal e-mail information, keeping it safe from unscrupulous people who might take your e-mail and spam you. Accuracy is key, because you will most likely be typing the ad and submitting it yourself. Any errors will be your own fault, so you won't get a replacement ad run for free. Check it twice to make sure you have it right, so that you can make that sale and collect that cash.

Flyers and Other Creative Ideas

A good old-fashioned flyer can still do the trick. Type one up, print off copies, and tack them all around town in places like gyms, daycare centers, and community centers. Many grocery stores have bulletin boards, and you can find other community bulletin boards around town. Remember to proofread, keep the flyer simple, and *always* put your contact information on it. Because you can't assume that readers will have a pen and paper handy, make it easy for potential buyers by reprinting your contact information over and over along the bottom of the flyer so that they can tear off a square and take it with them.

If your town allows this, you can park the item for sale right out on the front lawn and slap a big old "for sale" sign on it. Don't forget to use technology to your advantage by setting up a free text account with more information about the item, *any item*, for sale. Simply register for free at ForSalebyTxt.com. You'll enter the information and be assigned a text number. Then when a potential buyer texts your number, he or she will automatically receive more information about your item.

Swap Yourself Rich

Try This Cash-Free Way to Profit

Cash is great, but let's be honest, not everything you put up for sale will sell. Yet if you swap a sellable, it can still make you money. Basically, swapping is trading: giving someone something you don't use or love but that this person does want, in exchange for something he or she has that you do want and will use. As you pare down everything you own by half, keep in mind that you can swap just about anything.

Swapping can take place in person or online. I'll cover the pros and cons of both. Swapping something you don't use for something you will use or for points toward a future item is a great way not only to get what you need but also to get rid of something you don't. Although swapping won't bring in cold, hard cash, the way that selling an item will, it is still a really great option. Think about it. You get rid of something you aren't using and get something useful in return; someone else gets something he or she wants. It's a true win-win. No one had to pay a dime, and you avoid putting anything else in the landfills.

Here's the trick with swapping: you are swapping for things you *need* and will *use*. *Do not* swap for items you think are cute. You know what cute means: Can't Use This Ever. The trick is to use the right swapping site. Many sites focus on swapping books or CDs and DVDs, which I'll talk about later. If you swap a copy of *He's Just Not That into You* for a copy of *Slumdog Millionaire*, even though this type of entertainment will not get you more organized, you will save money. And if you swap for organizing solutions, products, and containers, you can purge the clutter and get items you need without spending a dime.

Swap Like a Pro

Now that you are ready to jump into the world of online swapping, here's how to be a pro. Before you list an item you'd be willing to swap, be clear about the approximate value so that you make a fair trade. Most likely, you would not want to swap twelve girls' dresses for one book. On the other hand, if it is a book you really want, you might be fine with the unequal dollar amount because the book has value in your eyes. Some easy ways to determine an item's approximate value include checking out sites such as Amazon.com or Shopping.Yahoo.com and even eBay.com. Remember, you want to make your item irresistible to a potential swapper. If you are going to post a photo, make it a decent one or don't do it at all. A bad photo is much worse than no photo at all. Be honest and accurate. You do not want to get a bad reputation as a swapper. So, if an item is slightly chipped, say so. No one likes to be surprised. Be a storyteller. Simply posting a few sentences about how you used and enjoyed the item or suggesting how someone else might use the item plants an idea about the possibilities in a reader's mind.

Top Twelve Swaps (Online or In Person)

1. Accessories
2. Books
3. CDs
4. Children's clothing
5. Costume jewelry
6. Craft supplies (yarn, material, etc.)
7. DVDs
8. Hodgepodge mix (figurines, photo frames, home décor items)
9. Jewelry (costume)
10. Movies
11. Unopened makeup and spa products
12. Video games

Best to Swap in Person

- Bakeware or small kitchen appliances
- Board games
- Children's toys
- Clothing
- Cookbooks
- Cookies (at holiday time)
- Coupons
- Exercise equipment
- Food (prepared in advance, frozen, and carefully labeled)
- Furniture
- Garden vegetables and fruits and flowers
- Gardening supplies
- Halloween costumes
- Home décor items (lamps, art, vases, figurines)

- Kitchen utensils
- Ornaments/holiday decorations
- Outdoor toys
- Purses and totes
- Recipes
- Scrapbooking supplies
- Seasonal decorations
- Shoes
- Sporting equipment
- Workshop items and tools (best as a co-ed swap)

Swap at Home, Wearing Your Pajamas

Online swapping allows you to reach swappers far and wide. There's no need to go out, hire a babysitter, or gas up the car. From the comfort of your own home, you can arrange a swap or two. Here are some of the most popular swap sites where you can swap a wide variety of items. There are also specific swap sites that focus solely on one or two items.

Web Site	The Good Stuff	The Not So Good Stuff	Your Cost
FreeUse.org	Easy to use.	Not available in all areas.	Free.
SwapatHome .com	You earn coupons when you swap, which can be used for items you want.	On the small side.	Free with one exception: you can add money to your account to get more coupons.

Web Site	The Good Stuff	The Not So Good Stuff	Your Cost
Swap-It-Now .com	This site calls itself the Internet's flea market. it's easy to browse and includes an estimate of the item's value.	On the small side.	Free.
SwapThing .com	A very large community with more than 3.5 million listings.	No rating system of members.	Free with one exception: you can add cash to a deal to even it out.
SwapTreasures .com	Well organized by category.	No rating system of members.	Free.
TradeAway.com	Barter-auction site for products and services.	Still growing in size.	The first listing is free, then you pay $9.95 for a 180-day membership.
TrashBank.com	Free trades with rating system.	The site mixes selling and swapping, so it can be confusing.	Free and paid.
Zwaggle.com	Large and well organized.	Focuses mostly on children's items.	Free: it works on a points system.

Do's and Don'ts of Online Swapping

Do check the item before listing it. Just because your margarita machine worked a year ago does not guarantee that it will work now; test items before you list them.

Do be upfront and honest about the condition of the item you are swapping. A fellow swapper may not mind that the cardigan you intend to swap is missing a button, but no one likes an unpleasant surprise. Be sure to mention any flaws when describing the item.

Do respond in a timely manner. Keep in mind that you are a member of a community and, as such, you have an obligation to reply, even if the answer is no. Be courteous; be as responsive as you'd want someone to be with you.

Do decline politely. If you are not interested, say that. There is no need to launch into a million reasons why, no need to justify why you're not interested, no need to insult the swapper. A courteous "no, thanks" will suffice.

Do swap fair. Swapping items of equal value keeps everyone happy. Otherwise, one side can start to feel taken advantage of and resentful of the swap. To avoid any conflict, keep swaps in the same price range.

Do keep it legal. Check the terms and conditions of the site; some sites and many states prohibit the transfer of tobacco, alcohol, lottery tickets, and other items. After you check the terms and conditions, if you still are not sure, then the answer is no. Better safe than sorry. And I'm sure it goes without saying, but here it is anyway: you must own the rights to the item you are swapping, which means no illegally copied material, no known knockoffs, or stolen items allowed.

Do resolve any disappointment prior to leaving negative feedback. Most of the time, each person is thrilled with his or her new swap item. If that is ever not the case, say something before you post negative feedback.

Do keep it safe. Overall, swappers are a kind bunch of people, but never forget you are dealing with people you do not know. Keep your personal information to yourself, and if you are meeting someone in person, ask him or her to meet you at work on your lunch break or at a local library or café to keep it safe.

Don't be a swapper stalker. Following up endlessly can be annoying. Although you would hope that the other person would respond to you, even if the answer is no, that is not always the case. A good rule of thumb is to follow up once; you can state that it will be your last follow-up e-mail. If you still don't hear back, assume that the answer is no and move on.

Don't delay getting it out the door. Keep in mind that someone is waiting for that item to arrive. If for any reason you are going to be delayed by more than twenty-four hours, let the other person know.

Don't swap underwear. Seriously, no one wants to swap for used undergarments. The same is true about items such as food, makeup, and fragrances. These are best listed *only* if they are new in the box, sealed, and otherwise untested.

Hosting a Successful Snack-'n-Swap Party

Swapping at home in your pajamas is not your only option. If you are looking for a great reason to socialize, then hosting a swap party just might be your thing. Swap parties are a great way to give your unwanted items to people who will use and love them. In exchange, you will get their unused stuff. The bonus is that you know who will get your things, so you can always borrow them back. Swaps provide an inexpensive and environmentally friendly way to update a wardrobe, make over a room, get new movies to watch, or trade in unwanted toys. Another benefit is that you can get rid of a bunch of items at once, which is less time-consuming than trying to dump each item individually. Also, there's no shipping charge.

Stop waiting to get invited to a swap party, and host your own. Recruit a co-host if you want some help. Now get ready to have some friends over and get some new stuff. Here are a few simple steps you can take to host a stress-free swap party.

Four weeks before your swap:

- Start a file to collect information all in one place.
- Pick your date, time, and theme and decide whether to allow kids and have a babysitter present.
- On your calendar, block out designated days before and after for prep and cleanup.
- Select your swappables.
- Write out your invitation list (3 to 20 people).
- Consider having a potluck swap, where guests bring swap items, a shopping bag, and snacks to share.

Two weeks before your swap:

- Send invitations using Pingg.com, Evite.com, or paper invitations. Include all of the following information:
  - The date, time, and location of the swap
  - A photo of your home
  - The theme of the event
  - An advance drop-off time
  - A regrets-only RSVP phone number and an e-mail address
- Your invitations should also mention these important ground rules:
  - All swappables must pass the sister-in-law test; if you would not give it to your sister-in-law, *don't* swap it.

- Unless swappers specify otherwise, unclaimed items will be donated to a designated charity. (If swappers want to keep their items, items must be clearly marked with the swapper's name. Use return address labels safety pinned to clothing and attach sticky notes in books.)

- Swappers should bring photos of items that are too large to carry into the swap. The photo must be marked with the swapper's contact information for item pickup.

- Be sure to specify whether kids will be allowed at the swap. (If you opt for a kid-friendly swap, set up a play zone away from the shopping area, and consider hiring a sitter to keep children occupied.)

One week before your swap:

- Start gathering these supplies:
  - Shopping bags
  - Bubble wrap or newspaper for fragile items
  - Extension cords and batteries for swappers to test electronics
  - Display tables
  - Full-length mirror (for clothing swaps)
  - Measuring tape
  - Rod or clothing line to hang items
  - Poker chips, which will be used as swapping currency

- Call your designated charity to arrange pickups if the leftover items are too big to drop off.

One day before your swap:

- Send e-mail reminders to your expected swappers.
- Prepare your display tables and rods or a clothesline for hanging.

- Make signs for display areas (for example, boys' clothes or DVDs).
- Speed clean whatever you can; swappers will be too busy to check for dust.
- Very important: Move your personal items out of the way so that they are not confused with swappables.
- Set up your display area like a store by grouping similar items and sorting by color and size.

The day of your swap:

- Tie a balloon to your mailbox or otherwise make your home easily identifiable.
- Put out drinks and snacks.
- Clear a space for people to move around while looking at or trying out items.
- Put out any latecomer items.
- Set up a kid-friendly zone (if you are having children attend).
- Welcome your guests.
- Allow one hour for swappers to check in their items. Give them poker chips that correspond to the item's value. They will use the chips like currency to "buy" the items they want.

  Color 1 = $25 or less

  Color 2 = $25 to $100

  Color 3 = $100 or more

- Allow a fifteen-minute preview window to peruse swappables.
- Allow a one-hour shop. (Draw names to determine the order, and each shopper can choose one item per turn.)
- Relax, enjoy the swap, and don't forget to shop for yourself.

The day after your swap:

- Clean up.

- Await the pickup of excess items by the charity or make the drop-off yourself. (Avoid the temptation to take anything out of the charity pile.)

Of course, hosting a swap party is just one way to go. Another is to have a swap with a group of people with whom you already get together on a regular basis, like your child's play group, a church group, or even your coworkers. Check out Meetup.com to see if there is a swap group running in your area already.

Swapping Skills and Labor

Do you enjoy cooking? Are you a super sewer? Swapping talents, also known as bartering, is another way to go. Are you looking to work with an organizer, but you don't want to lay out the cash? No problem. Swap a few hours of organizing time for something you can offer that a local organizer wants. Swap cleaning for tailoring, yoga classes for tutoring—you name it, and chances are you can find someone to swap with.

I swapped a professional photo shoot for organizing services. My headshots came out wonderful, and my photographer's daughter got a newly organized bedroom. You can find lots of options on sites such as BarterPlanet.com, BizXchange.com, Baby sitterExchange.com, FavorPals.com, and U-Exchange.com.

Online Borrowing from Virtual Friends and Neighbors

A recent study found that 80 percent of the things we own are used fewer than one time per month. Come on, fess up. If you own a bike, when is the last time you went for a ride? If the tires are flat and the seat has a layer of dust on it, then it might make sense to rent one for the day that you need it. Maybe it will take a little more effort, but I'll bet the extra hundreds of dollars in savings in your pocket will make it worthwhile. Sure, you know you can borrow books and even movies and music from the library. But you can also borrow so much more than that from places other than the library. These days, you can use items and return them by renting or borrowing things such as a weed whacker, a bicycle, and even a car.

Although swapping is a really great way to save money, sometimes you don't need to get something in return. That's when borrowing makes the most sense. Let's say that you need to snake out the kitchen drain. You could hire a plumber, whose prices probably start at $75 just to walk in your front door. You could drive to the local home improvement store and purchase a snake for more than $100 that you'll most likely use only that one time. Or you could pay a small rental fee or maybe even borrow it for free. I like the free option. With just a little bit of research, you can see whether what you need is out there. You'll save money and avoid having to store it, plus it's one less thing that will end up in the landfill. Neighborrow.com is a great site for borrowing lots of stuff. Do you prefer to borrow items from a small group of good friends and neighbors? Start a list on a Web site such as Whiteboard.com, which everyone in the group can have access to. Then people can add the items that they are offering to others to borrow and can make notes about who borrowed and returned which items.

Reading Your Way to Riches

It just so happens that one of my sisters and I like to read the same authors and many of the same magazines. We split our book collection and magazine subscriptions between us.

That way, we spend half the amount of money and use half the storage space. To keep it simple, I buy every other book that comes out, and she purchases those that alternate with mine. We each subscribe to a few magazines. The best part of it is that because we each know the other person is waiting to read a book or magazine, we don't let them linger on our to-read piles.

Flowers for All

My father, Jim, and his wife, Stacey, live next door to Fenn's Flower Barn and Greenhouse. When they were planning their wedding, they wanted homegrown flowers for their reception. They borrowed some greenhouse space to grow their own flowers. Over the years, they've contributed to the flower shop, and, in return, they get to pick a basket or two of fresh strawberries, which is a win-win for each side.

Libraries Aren't Just for Books Anymore

Some libraries lend much more than books or movies. You can often you borrow:

- Cake pans
- Camping equipment
- Computer games
- Crafting supplies
- DVDs
- Framed art prints
- Music
- Sporting equipment
- Tools
- Toys
- Video cameras

Where to Rent Items

You can rent the following items from these Web sites:

Almost Anything

  Zilok.com

  Loanables.com

Bikes

  iBike.org

Black Tie Apparel

  OneNightAffair.com

Cars

  Zipcar.com

  Hertz.com

Designer Handbags

  BagBorrowSteal.com

Jewelry

  BorrowedBling.com

Wedding Dresses

  WeddingDressMarket.com

Spend Thirty Days
with Jamie

P repare for your big money marathon by finding a tote
bag, such as a canvas bag, and put a kitchen timer, and
a pen and paper in it. Now you are ready.

So, how much money are you looking to walk away with at
the end of our time together? Write the number in your half-
and-half journal so that we can track your progress. And
remember, life can happen, interrupting the best-laid plans.
So if you miss a day, jump back in where you left off.

Day 1

Log onto AnnualCreditReport.com, select your state, and pull
your credit report for *free* from one of the three credit reporting agencies. Print the report and review it for inaccuracies.

Incorrect information on your credit report could be costing you. Many auto insurers factor in your credit score into your insurance rates, and credit card companies can use it to determine your interest rate. But nowadays, your credit rating has numerous applications, which are not always financial.

Label a file folder "current credit report," and file the report in your file box. In most states each of the three reporting agencies allows you one free report per year, so request your report every four months to keep a handle on the current state of your credit. On your calendar, mark the dates four and eight months from now when you will need to pull your report again. Include your user name and password for AnnualCreditReport.com on the calendar so you won't waste time searching for them when it is time to log on again.

Day 2

Bring on the competition. Flip through your stack of junk mail to see what offers you've received from competitive utilities or credit card companies. Then call your current company, ask for the retention department, and explain that you'd like to remain a loyal customer, but in order for you to do so, you will need the company to match the offer made by its competition. Wouldn't it be worth a few minutes on the phone to save $15 to $30 a month?

Day 3

Borrow some money. I'm not kidding; borrowing books and other items from the library can add up to big savings. So, when is the last time you used your library card? You can't remember? Get it out and check whether it has expired. If so, renew it.

What's that, you don't have a library card? No problem, head on over to the library and get one. Even if you opt to borrow instead of buy three hardcover books from the library, you've saved about $70. You can also use the library to preview books before you buy them. If you really love it, get one of your own. Often, you'll find out that you really don't want a copy for your own library (unless it is one of my books, of course).

Day 4

Send out a search party to retrieve your latest credit card statement from the pile of mail and papers. Scan the charges for accuracy. Although you may not have time to match every receipt to every line on the statement, you'll be able to spot an accidental double billing, an unknown charge, a subscription charge you can cancel, or fees being charged for credit protection that you may not want or need or even know you had. You may even spot one of the newest fees being charged: the one for not opting to go green and still receiving paper statements, which can be anywhere from $2.50 to $5 per statement.

Day 5

You undoubtedly have at least one gift card or store credit lying around somewhere, waiting to be used. Dig it out right now, place it in your wallet, and leave yourself a reminder note to stop at the store or shop online in the next week to use that coupon. If you don't need to purchase anything for yourself at the moment, look ahead on the calendar to see what occasions are coming up, so that you can buy something for someone's birthday, a holiday, or another special event.

Day 6

DIY—no, really, do it yourself. What repair or upgrade are you considering hiring someone to complete? Faux painting the bathroom, fixing a tile in the kitchen, hanging a chandelier, or maybe fixing a leaky faucet? Before you call in the professionals, check out your local home improvement store. It just might be hosting a free clinic on the topic. Sit through the class to see whether you can learn to do it yourself. If so, you've saved yourself a bundle. If not, you at least learned how not to get taken advantage of when you're negotiating the price, plus you most likely received a nice store coupon for attending the clinic.

Day 7

Print money. Well, it's almost like printing money if you change the setting on your computer printer to fast draft. This uses a lot less ink and prints a heck of a lot faster. When you print something superimportant, such as a photo, you can return to the regular print setting. But until you get to the very end of the print cartridge, chances are you won't even be able to notice the difference—in the quality, that is. You will certainly notice that you are replacing the cartridges a lot less often.

Day 8

Sing in the shower. The longer you stand under the warm water, the more money runs down the drain. Sure, sometimes you need that long relaxing shower, but more often than not, you are simply in the habit of taking a long shower. The next time you hop in, time yourself to see how long your shower really is. You might be surprised. Then set a timer for your average time minus five minutes, and challenge yourself to see whether you can shower before the timer buzzes.

Day 9

Look under the couch cushion; there's probably money hiding under it. Collect loose change in a single spot; the most practical location is near the front door, where you can dump it on your way into the house. When the container is full, don't waste your time rolling coins in wrappers. There are places you can go to cash in your change without having to waste hours sorting those coins. Then take your coins to the bank and deposit the cash. Now, instead of accidentally sucking up your money with the vacuum cleaner or letting coins sit in stacks on the dresser, you can put your loose change to good use.

Day 10

Don't let your money run down the drain. During a rainstorm, a lot of water runs off your driveway and sidewalks. Put that water to work for you by setting up a rain barrel, a simple container to collect the water, which you can then use to water your plants, flowers, and garden. Or you can even use the water for your fish tank. If you can't set up a rain barrel, no problem. How about reusing the water from the dehumidifier or placing a small bucket in the shower to collect the extra water?

Day 11

Light up your savings. How many times have you heard that you should swap out your lightbulbs? How many times have you thought about doing it? Have you ever wondered whether it makes more sense to wait until the old-style bulbs burn out or to replace them now? The answer is that replacing them all now is the best money-saving and planet-saving option. Simply replacing your incandescent lightbulbs with CFL bulbs can add up to big savings. On average, CFL bulbs use 75 percent less electricity, which equates to 10,000 hours, rather than 1,500, per bulb.

Day 12

Place a kitchen timer near the computer, and use it the next time you log on. Just set the timer for ten minutes before you start checking your e-mail or doing a Web search. The ticking timer will keep you focused on the task so that you waste less time, which, in and of itself, is a good thing. But it also means you are reading fewer advertisements for items that you may be tempted to buy. Less time shopping online adds up to more time and money saved.

Day 13

Be flexible. Have you signed up for the flexible spending account (FSA) option through your employer? If not, you might want to. It takes pretax dollars and sets them aside for your health-care expenses. If you have an FSA, check to see the remaining balance, and be sure to schedule appointments to use up the money before you lose it.

Day 14

Unplug everything that glows. The light on the microwave, the Internet modem, and even the television when it's turned off still draw electricity, running up your bill. Unplug them or put them on a single power strip that you can shut down.

Day 15

Take advantage of free money. Do you have any idea how many free events are taking place in your own backyard? From plays in the park to festivals, to workshops, to classes. Check out the local paper and the online community calendar, or do an online search for "free + [your zip code]" to see what pops up. The first free event you can mark on your calendar is my next free monthly Moneyize Group phone call.

Day 16

Pay your bills online. You'll save time and money, avoid postage fees, and will be less likely to overlook a due date. You can even automate the payments by having the money drafted directly from your bank account or paying by credit card. If you are uncomfortable with the idea of money being debited directly from your account, you can open a checking account for the sole purpose of bill paying and transfer only the money needed to pay bills into the account so that there is no risk of mistaken debits. At the very least, sign up for alerts from your creditors so that they can send you a reminder e-mail when a payment is due.

Day 17

Fix a drip or add weather stripping. Water dripping down the drain is the same as money washing down the pipes. Gaps around doors let the air escape, raising your energy bills even higher. Fix these issues with two quick and inexpensive fixes: add weather stripping around the door frame to keep the outdoors out. A little plumber's tape around the faucet should do the trick for the drip.

Day 18

Program your savings. Change to a programmable thermo-stat that will allow you to keep the temperature at a higher or lower level when you are not home, saving you money on your energy bill.

Day 19

Get audited. An energy audit, which is usually conducted by your local utility company, at no charge, gives you a report suggesting no- and low-cost fixes to save energy and your money at the same time.

Day 20

Try the store-brand version of an item on your shopping list. Many times, items come from the same plant but are simply packaged differently, one for the high-end brand and one for the store brand. You may find that you like the store brand as much or even more than the higher-priced item.

Day 21

Got baking soda? We've all heard of the multitudes of ways we can clean and freshen our homes with an item right out of our pantry, such as baking soda, vinegar, and lemons, but how many of us are actually whipping up our own homemade cleaning concoctions? Not only can these homemade cleaners be easy on your budget, but they are also good for your home and the earth. Hop online and do a quick search for homemade cleaners, and pick one to try. Then spend a few minutes creat-ing the cleaner. You'll find that most of them clean as well as, or even better than, the commercial brands. I post my favorite tried-and-true recipes on my Web site. I would love to hear your own recipes.

Day 22

Filter your funds. Changing water filters, plus filters on water heaters and air conditioners, means that these appliances will function more effectively and save you energy and money. Because most filters require only a yearly change, mark your calendar as a reminder to do it again next year, along with the model number, so that you know exactly which filters you need to buy.

Day 23

Watch less television. You'll save time and energy, lowering your electricity bill. Plus, you'll view fewer commercials, which means you won't be tempted to buy things you see on the commercials. Try substituting a one-hour show with one hour of game time with your family.

Day 24

Ticket your money. Do you want to spend a day at the museum? How about a night at the theater? Want to hit the water park? Before you purchase those tickets, take a moment to check with your bank or your utility company. At least one of them is likely to have a partnership with the attraction you want to buy tickets for, and you can get a steep discount or maybe even get admitted for free. No kidding, the first week-end of every month I can walk into the Liberty Science Center for zip-zero-zilch-nada, providing that I show the center my

Bank of America credit card. And I can bring the family, provided that each member has a BOA credit card, and you bet they do. In a four-minute phone call to the bank, I added them as authorized users on my account and had cards sent to me—score! The amount saved: $17 per person. And I save $5 per ticket to the local water park simply for picking up a coupon at the bank. I get into the annual balloon festival for half price just for buying my tickets at the local quick mart, and I picked up half-price Broadway tickets at the library.

Utility companies, convenience stores, libraries, banks, and your human resources department at work often have these agreements with local attractions. If you are a member of an organization or an association such as AAA and AARP, mention this when you check out. Often, simply by being a member you are granted a discount. Every little bit helps.

Day 25

Check the benefits of the memberships you have with organizations like AAA or AARP as well as the benefits offered by your company and your credit cards. Some have reciprocal memberships that could save you money or maybe cancel out another membership that you have. For example, I have free towing within 100 miles with my platinum business card and a professional membership that offers me trip maps, so I was able to suspend my AAA membership.

Day 26

Do you need expert advice? Are you stumped by a legal or tax question? Before you shell out money for a paid consultation, take a look online. Although online help is not always a substitute for a paid consultation, many times you can get the answer you need or at least determine whether an in-person consult is necessary. Check out sites such as Score.org for all sorts of business-related questions and IRS.gov for tax questions or call the Internal Revenue Service directly (1-800-829-1040). It has operators on call who can answer a myriad of tax questions.

Try message boards that specialize in the topic that's of interest to you. I have my own message board, "Real Organizing for Real People," online at iVillage.com, where you can post photos of the space you're planning to organize. I will reply with an organizing plan to help you. There are expert advice sites covering thousands of topics, such as AllExperts.com, and don't overlook online article databanks like Ezine.com or HubPages.com. Online legal help at FreeAdvice.com and sometimes just a good old-fashioned Google search will net you the results you've been after.

Day 27

Bag up some savings. We've all made an impulse purchase or picked up something only to get home to find out we had one already. Instead of keeping it, dig out the receipt and make the return. If it is more than $5, then it'll be worth the return trip to the store the next time you are in the area. The only catch is, get your money and leave. Don't pick up something else that catches your eye.

Day 28

List your savings. Decide that from here on out, you will *shop only from a list*. This one change alone can save you thousands, I'm not exaggerating, I mean *thousands* of dollars. There'll be no more trying to guess whether you need toothpaste or printer ink. Your list will reveal everything. Choose a single notebook to jot down your lists, then give your notebook a home so that you can always find it again when you need it. Grab it when you head out to the store, unless you are keeping it in your bag. Then you'll have it no matter where you are. Write the list, grouping similar items together: keep grocery items together, office items in another part, and pet care items in yet another. That way, when you are in a store, you can see what you need at a glance.

Day 29

Dine and divide your bucks. Are you heading out to dinner? When you get there, try this: order an appetizer to share and then a single entrée to split. Not only will this be a healthier portion size, but it is also healthier for your wallet. For even more savings, have an appetizer at home and go out for the entrée or buy a whole cake for the cost of one pricey slice and eat your sweets at home.

Day 30

Pop online and check out upcoming classes at your local community college or adult community school. There just may be a class for free or at a low cost to replace something you're paying full price for. You might be able to replace a gym membership with an exercise class series, or you can take a cooking class to learn how to make lower-cost versions of some of the dishes that you eat in restaurants in your very own kitchen.

Conclusion

Change Your Habits, Change Your Life

Congratulations! Can you hear me cheering for you? I'm so proud of you for sticking with the half-and-half organizing system. It's been a pleasure joining you on your journey to clear the clutter and stash the cash. So, how does it feel? Do you feel lighter? More in control? Happier? And how much more money do you have? Did you meet or exceed your goal?

Let's just pause for a moment so that you can think about what an important turning point this is for you. You broke old clutterbug habits and embraced a new way of living. You stuck with it, even when it was not easy or comfortable. You didn't give up or get lazy or sidetracked. You held yourself accountable, and your reward will be leading a rich life in *all* areas but, especially, enjoying financial health and happiness.

Now is a perfect time to retake the CAM Quiz on page 14 to get an updated score. We'd expect you to score higher this time around, although you might not if you are still enacting the principles. Mark your calendar to see how far you've come in just three months, and don't forget to log your results in your half-and-half journal. In fact, keep your journal handy and refer to it often, reading past entries and adding dollar sign moments as you come across them.

Think back to where you were when you started, how you felt, how much more clutter and how much less cash you had. Return to page 80, where you answered questions relating to how you felt about the current state of your home and life. Now see how you feel today.

Are you wondering what happened to some of my most memorable clients?

Jennifer has remained Boyd's Bear–free. She now vacations with ease, having pared down her closet and made lots of cash.

Kristin has pared down her wedding gifts to only the ones she and her husband love or use, and they no longer rent storage.

Tracey takes great pride in the organizing habits she is passing down to her children, with the knowledge that they will not need to hire me when they get older.

Maryann now has an empty, but organized, nest. She and her husband have regular office-organizing dates, followed by a fun date. And they have released the guilt they felt about having three homes.

Once again, I congratulate you for taking this journey. You now have all the tools you need to become and stay clutter-free, as well as financially healthy and happy. I am honored to have accompanied you, and nothing will make me prouder than to see you continue down this path. Remember, this is your shot to create the life you dream of, and good for you for taking it! I can't wait for you to contact me with your success story.

As you continue to take what you've learned and implement it in your day-to-day life, I'd like to leave you with some principles for lasting success, to make sticking to your new path easier. Mark this page and read these principles often until you know them by heart.

Your Ten Moneyize Principles for Lasting Success

1. Filling an inner need with an outer item is never a long-term solution.

Buying things just to feel important, fill a void, or get out of the house actually only compounds the problem. It's a vicious cycle. You have too many possessions, so you lack time, space, energy, and money, which makes you feel bad about yourself. So you buy more to feel better, which only leaves you with more stuff to feel bad about. Get off the merry-go-round of accumulating stuff. Enlist the help of a friend who can talk you out of the shoe department. Retail therapy is never a solution.

2. Objects never provide lasting memories, but experiences and connections always do.

Don't become overly attached to material things. The relationships in your life are much more valuable, and be sure to spend time appreciating them.

My mom, Sue, unexpectedly fell ill and passed away from lung cancer, even though she was not a smoker. I barely had time to comprehend what her doctor was telling me before she was gone. I couldn't even tell you what she bought me every year for my birthday; the memories of our time together are much more valuable. The one thing I wish for is more time with her. I remember some of the best conversations we had as we strolled along the sidewalk on our evening walks, exchanging stories about our days, talking out problems, laughing over funny incidents, and sharing our dreams.

I know that not everyone has that sort of relationship with his or her mom, and I consider myself lucky. In fact, I'd say my mom was my best friend; she was the first person I called when I had good news to share and I credit her with passing down so many of the reuse, renew, and repurpose ideas that I teach people.

3. The more you own, the less money, time, energy, space, and connection to others you have.

For each item you let into your home, you lose something else. Even one little item, such as a new black skirt, seems harmless enough, but in just a matter of minutes it can start to take over your life. You need to take it out of the bag; now you have another bag to deal with. Then you have to use water to wash it and put it away in your closet. Good luck finding a hanger. Once it is hung up, it is taking up space where something you already owned was supposed to go, so something else got displaced.

4. Items have power—use caution.

Those books, those jeans, that piece of paper all wield power over your existence. They can either enhance your life, making it richer, or they can damage your well-being and your bank account. Think of a single small recipe clipped from a magazine. Seemingly inconsequential in nature, this little square of paper can stop you in your tracks. Should you keep it, should you store it away, and if so, how? These questions can cause you to become overwhelmed. The decisions are great, the possibilities are endless, and so, yes, items have the power to control you.

5. Items keep you rooted in a place and a time, not allowing you the time, space, and energy to move forward.

Not only does clutter make you poor, but it also keeps you from being able to move forward. It's impossible to find the energy to do fun or new things. It's difficult to find the time to enjoy life. And it is hard to have room in your life to relax when clutter surrounds you.

6. Objects hold no memories; the memory is inside of you.

There are no memories inside inanimate objects, much as you might like to imagine that your teddy bear really heard all of those stories you shared while growing up. Sure, seeing an item might trigger the memory, but you can always take a photo of the item to have the same effect.

Remember, the souvenir from your last cruise, the sweater your mom loved to wear, and your child's first pair of shoes are not full of memories. You are!

7. An item on sale is rarely a bargain, and a free item is never truly free.

You know the kind of stuff I mean; you pick it up just because it is on sale, not because you need it. Or you buy it only to get the free item that accompanies the purchase. I'm in the middle of receiving a cooking magazine subscription that I fell for just because it came with a free tote bag. The tote bag ended up being too small to be functional.

8. Upgrades are not automatic.

Think before you upgrade. You are not automatically entitled to get the best, newest, coolest, most up-to-date version of anything. If you need a cell phone, then you need a cell phone. Just because a newer model is introduced does not mean you *have* to get it. You may *want* it, but you certainly don't *need* it if the phone you already own still works.

9. The price tag does not tell the whole story.

There is so much more to owning an item than simply bringing it home. Think of belongings as if they were an adopted puppy or a cute kitten. Sure, it looks innocent enough, and you pay a fee to bring it home. But then what? There are vet bills, food, walks, toys, and so much more. The same is true for items: once you get them home, there's storage, caring for them, and so on. Maybe you bought a cute silver charm necklace. Remember, CUTE stands for "Can't Use This Ever!" So, now you have yet another necklace, probably similar to one you already own. Regardless of the price tag, you now need to find space for it in your jewelry box, and you have to buy jewelry cleaner. Then you need to find room to store the jewelry cleaner. Plus, you have to spend time polishing the necklace, and on and on. You get the idea, right?

10. Your clutter and your bank balance increase or decrease according to how closely your actions match your values.

You know that the less clutter you have, the richer you are. So, you say you want a richer life, and with each moment you have the choice to either align your next action with that statement or not. Choose wisely, and if you make a misstep, forgive yourself and move on.

Finally, this is not a one-shot deal. You are bound to accumulate more stuff, so mark your calendar now and join me again in one year for a mini toss-it challenge. You want to keep up with the new stuff that's coming in and the items that no longer suit you. Your first time is usually when you find the big, big bucks, but that doesn't mean you shouldn't continue to pare down and bank money. I'll see you in a year!

Index